THE POSY BOOK

THE POSY BOOK

Garden-Inspired Bouquets That Tell a Story

With a Modern Floral Dictionary

TERESA H. SABANKAYA

FOREWORD BY AMY STEWART

Photographs by Danyelle Dee

Illustrations by Maryjo Koch

The Countryman Press

A division of W. W. Norton & Company

Independent Publishers Since 1923

For information about permission to reproduce selections from this book, write to
Permissions, The Countryman Press, 500 Fifth Avenue, New York, NY 10110

For information about special discounts for bulk purchases, please contact W. W. Norton
Special Sales at specialsales@wwnorton.com or 800-233-4830

Manufacturing through Asia Pacific Offset
Book design by Seton Rossini
Production manager: Devon Zahn

The Countryman Press
www.countrymanpress.com

A division of W. W. Norton & Company, Inc.
500 Fifth Avenue, New York, NY 10110
www.wwnorton.com

978-1-68268-263-0

10 9 8 7 6 5 4 3 2 1

Yes, flowers have their language. Theirs is an oratory that speaks in perfumed silence, and there is tenderness, and passion, and even the lightheartedness of mirth, in the variegated beauty of their vocabulary. To the poetical mind, they are not mute to each other; to the pious, they are not mute to their Creator; and ours shall be the office, in this little volume, to translate their pleasing language, and to show that no spoken word can approach to the delicacy of sentiment to be inferred from a flower reasonably offered; that the softest impressions may be thus conveyed without offense, and even profound grief alleviated, at a moment when the most tuneful voice would grate harshly on the ear, and when the stricken soul can be soothed only by unbroken silence.

—FREDERIC SHOBERL, LOUISE CORTAMBERT, AND LOUIS-AIMÉ MARTIN, *The language of flowers: with illustrative poetry*, 1848

CONTENTS

FOREWORD
BY AMY STEWART

When I met Teresa Sabankaya fifteen years ago, she was working out of a kiosk on Santa Cruz's Pacific Avenue. I've never seen a more exuberant flower shop, or a smaller one: from a workroom not much larger than a telephone booth, Teresa snipped stems, wrapped bouquets, and coaxed fragile, seasonal blooms into heartfelt arrangements. All around her, on the sidewalk, a dazzling array of fresh-picked dahlias, sunflowers, lilies, and sweet peas enticed passersby.

And it was impossible, really, to pass the shop by. Even in those days, before every experience went straight to Instagram, people stopped to gawk and take pictures. Everything Teresa had on offer was, in some way, unusual: jars of blowsy, wildly fragrant garden roses on short stems, tiny bright bluebells that belonged in an English meadow, and stalks of lilac that would only be on the market for three weeks, because their season was so fleeting.

Anyone who stopped long enough would meet Teresa herself, who would appear with pruning shears in one hand and silk ribbon in the other, plus a sunny smile and a gracious Texas accent. She'd tell you about the origins of her flowers—many came from her own garden, and some from fellow gardeners who would just drive up with buckets of blooms in the backseat—and then she'd introduce you to their hidden histories and meanings. An herb for compassion, a budded branch for hope, a sprig of tiny blooms for affection.

I learned from Teresa to choose my flowers by occasion. Rather than ask for a dozen roses, or a bouquet in pink and yellow, I would tell her, "I need a bouquet for a rather elegant executive who's retiring," or "I'd like something for a friend expecting her first baby." What Teresa came up with was always wonderfully handmade, one-of-a-kind, and perfect for the occasion.

A posy invites scrutiny. It asks for a little attention, a bit of consideration. A posy is small enough to hold between the palms, but it delivers a world of sentiment. By reviving the lost art of sending messages in the form of a nosegay, Teresa manages to do something more than sell a pretty, perishable product. She puts her heart into it, too.

Now, with the same generosity of spirit that inspired her to launch her flower shop, Teresa has woven her wisdom, spirit, and artistry into this beautiful book. In these pages you'll see that anyone can make a posy. Like a favorite recipe, it's meant to be savored and shared. I hope you'll be inspired to try it yourself, and to welcome a bit of floral enchantment into your life.

A POSY FOR YOU

My Valentine
Rose, *true love*
Hypericum, *protection*
Ranunculus, *rich in charms*
radiant with charms
Oregano, *happiness*
Hypericum, *protection*
Veronica, *female fidelity*
Leucodendron, *loyalty*
Dusty Miller, *felicity*

ACKNOWLEDGMENTS

The greatest influence and inspiration for me to write this book *came* from a book. It was a book that I bought back in 1994, titled *Tussie-Mussies—The Victorian Art of Expressing Yourself in the Language of Flowers,* written by Geraldine Adamich Laufer. I kept this book in my nightstand, and over the course of several years I would retrieve it and thumb through the pages. Looking at these pretty little nosegays made me feel so romantic, and so nostalgic for a long-ago time when folks were sentimental about things like nature and flowers. The idea that each of the flowers, plants, and herbs used in these tussie-mussies had a meaning attached to it captivated me. And each tussie had a line drawn from the flower, leaf, or herb with an explanation as to what kind of plant it was, and its definition in the language of flowers. This book made me realize that I see these flowers growing along the roadside all the time! The wild hazel growing along my country road had such powerful meanings: *poetic inspiration, meditation, knowledge* . . . and it made me wonder why on earth don't we use flowers to communicate our most intricate messages anymore?

Through the years, I have collected *many* books on the language of flowers and they have all inspired me each in their own way. Some are vintage, with very old pages tattered and worn from being thumbed through by countless hands. The bindings are soft and worn and the delicate pages hint of their long-gone gilt edges. These books take me back in time and I enjoy the feeling I get as I submerge myself into the forgotten world of coded floral messages. I feel the company of earlier owners as I hold each book gently, turning the pages ever so carefully. I wonder about the books' now-departed owners; who were they? And were they as charmed by this mystical and magical language as I am? My gratitude is boundless to all those before me who have written about the language of flowers and floral symbolism—thank you for influencing me to write this book.

I owe tremendous gratitude to Debra Prinzing, who is my friend and colleague. Debra is a writer, speaker, founder of Slow Flowers™, and a leading advocate for American-grown flowers. In 2015, Debra was visiting me, staying in my little garden guesthouse. I had been thinking of writing a book about posies and the language of flowers for some time already, but I wanted her opinion on the idea. I made a sweet posy for her to "test the waters," and I left it by her bedside in the little cottage, awaiting her arrival. The posy I gifted

to Debra wasn't by any means the first posy I had ever created and gifted to someone, but it was the posy that would be the determining factor on whether I should pursue the book idea—or not! Well, Debra adored the posy, and she loved the idea of incorporating it into modern floral design, especially in a book.

I am eternally indebted to Amy Stewart. Amy is the *New York Times*–bestselling author of numerous books, including *Flower Confidential* (2007), in which I was featured. Amy wrote about my unique-at-the-time practice of growing my own flowers to use in floral design at my retail flower shop. The *Flower Confidential* book and Amy were instrumental in catapulting me out of the shadows and casting some much-needed light on the worldwide, multibillion-dollar flower business. It was because of Amy and her book that I was able to cross paths with Debra Prinzing. They are both extraordinary women, and I am so blessed to call them my friends today. My heartfelt appreciation to them both for their continued belief in me. I cherish our friendships beyond words.

And not with any less emphasis, much gratitude and love go to my family. My husband is my best friend, and without his love, friendship, and support in so many ways, I wouldn't have been able to write this book. The entire Sabankaya family—with the lovely compound on which the garden of my dreams sits—all have been instrumental in the development of this book.

My daughter Alania is my most spirited cheerleader, not only in this endeavor but in all that I do. She is the epitome of pure sweetness and love—thank you. My daughter Antalia, whose emphathy, soul, and passion always astounds me and teaches me every day—thank you. I thank God for both of you.

My mom and dad, and their partners in life—your love and guidance throughout my life made me who I am today. Thank you for that. My two sisters and their families—I love you all more than words can say. I am so blessed to have you on my side and giving me the juju to get this done. You help to shape the lives of my children, and your support and love is my lifeblood.

Dawn, the queen of my flower girls—and all the Doon Crew. You are all I can ever ask for. You have filled some tall orders and always have my back. Thank you for your love and support.

And finally, my circle of friends—you know who you are! You've all been anchors for me. Thanks for swooping me away to lunch breaks and cocktail hours. It's good to keep a nice balance!

INTRODUCTION

Do you remember the first time you received flowers? More than likely you do, and you undoubtedly remember how it made you feel, too. There is nothing that makes you feel more loved and cared for than a gift of flowers. And what if the flowers we give and receive from one another conveyed sentiments using the language of flowers? How wonderful to receive flowers that are not only beautiful to look at but carry a secret message for you as well. Flowers express meanings and sentiments, and if you let them, they can speak *to* you as the recipient, or *for* you as the giver. And there is a whole world of this extraordinary language, with a wide array of sentiments that are well within your reach, waiting for you to discover.

Because of my undying fascination with flowers and their language, this has been an easy research subject for me. I have been able to gain some knowledge on the topic, but *(disclaimer approaching!)* I am not a historical scholar, nor do I have a formal education in botany. With this book, my intention is to inspire you and to impart the simple knowledge that flowers have captivated us for centuries, and they have played some role in symbolic, religious, medicinal, and celebratory rituals for many cultures throughout history. One such role is in the posy, a small bouquet of flowers chosen for their meanings. *By creating a sentiment using the language of flowers, a posy can serve as a vehicle to convey profound messages that sometimes cannot be articulated in words.*

Floriography—the cryptologic communication through the use or arrangement of flowers—has been around since the nineteenth century. But today we have all but forgotten about the historical language of flowers, and we rarely, if ever, use this language while gifting and using flowers. Why is it that we barely acknowledge the idea that flowers, plants, and even trees have a hidden language? A language that once held a significant place in the daily lives of people?

We are living in an age of technological wonder, and things are moving at a fast pace. And we are busier than ever before. Who has time for this? But I mean, really, it's a cool concept—a secret language and sentiment, presented with beautiful flowers to the ones you love, your friends, your neighbor, your coworkers, or anyone you want to impress, and all without saying a word. I believe we *do* have time for this, and we should certainly create the time for this. The flowers are already out there for us—at farmer's markets, the supermarket, the florist, and especially in your own garden. And all you have to do is learn to use them to express your sentiments, your thoughts, or any specific message you want to send with them. This book is written to make it easy for you to learn about the language of flowers and how to use it in these modern times. Here, you'll find instructions on how to make your own posies coupled with a modern language of flowers dictionary, and by using these as guides, you'll be able to select flowers, plants, and herbs to create garden-inspired bouquets with meaning—also known as posies.

There are many language of flowers dictionaries available today—some are very old, and some more recent. While the older language of flowers books contain many definitions, they lack the meanings of some of our modern hybrids of plants, trees, and flowers. And there are some references to plants that many of us are not familiar with, and some that may never have even existed at all. The recent language of flowers books, all gloriously beautiful and inspiring, usually lack an all-inclusive dictionary. I believe part of the reason we rarely use the language of flowers when we give floral gifts is because we lack a modernized and comprehensive reference as to what flowers mean, including the new ones that we see often, either in our own gardens or in public places, or at the nursery, that do not have a meaning attached to them. We also lack a modernized floral arrangement to herald the language of flowers. And that's where this book comes into play.

The Posy Book holds a modern floral dictionary—a comprehensive compilation of many historical language of flowers dictionaries and other references—that also includes names and descriptions of some very old flowers and plants that we're not familiar with today. For instance, the gillyflower, which historically referenced a spicy-scented flower. Did you know the gillyflower can be either a carnation, wallflower, or stock? And that the gillyflower can encode different messages according to the color and the shape of the petals? The dictionary also includes new plant and flower introductions or "inductees," which may be my favorite thing about the dictionary overall! During the last hundred years or so, we have hybridized new flowers and plants that lend themselves nicely to posies, but we haven't been able to use them in floriography because there was no definition in any existing language of flowers dictionary or reference book. With this updated dictionary, we now have an extensive reference to create sentiments in flowers, the modern way—with a posy!

This is a different kind of language of flowers book. In addition to the modern floral dictionary, I've included extensive instructions and resources to help you actually use the language of flowers today. And my aim is to make you feel like you *should* be using the forgotten language of flowers. I want to create a new language of flowers phenomenon! Inside are detailed portraits of beautiful posies, each with their own recipes for the portrayal of many different sentiments. To help you jump right in and make your own, there is the *Quick-Start Occasions Directory* (page 237), where all you need to do is select the occasion that you'd like to make a posy for, and the chart will guide you to select a few flowers, or even just one, to create a posy based on that occasion. There is also a *Quick-Start Sentiments Directory* (page 239), which you can scan for a feeling or emotion to find a list of some of the flowers and plant materials that portray it. And of course, you can always go directly to the extensive *New Language of Flowers Dictionary* to explore and create your posy based on your own choice of flowers and their meanings (page 151).

There is also a resource directory to help you gather all your materials—everything you need to get started. A detailed and step-by-step instruction section will make you feel confident right off the bat, and if you follow the simple tips I have included, you can skip over years of trial and error! There is a resource directory for cut flowers and plants, both from the garden and from other outlets, and there are sources listed for when you want to get crafty with your sentiment tags too, as well as sources for the perfect posy containers. And one of the best and most handy resources is *The Posy Book*'s own downloadable and customizable sentiment tags from my website, teresasabankaya.com. It's all here, ready for you to put to good use.

By using this book for your inspiration, instruction, and reference, you will be an expert posy-maker in no time. What a hit you'll be with the people you make posies for! And always remember, flowers are not just a pretty face in the field, garden, or vase—they are a beautiful method of communicating and articulating feelings and emotions that sometimes cannot be eloquently spoken. Through creating a beautiful, intentional floral composition, you participate in a wonderful way to portray a feeling you have for another person: to depict a sense of sorrow for a loss, or to congratulate an engagement, celebrate a birthday, or to just say you care.

A Posy Primer

THE FARMER-FLORIST, THE POSY, AND HOW IT REALLY DID BEGIN IN THE GARDEN

On a fall day in 1999, while my youngest daughter attended her first day at preschool and my older daughter entered the first grade, I sat with my girlfriend on the edge of a two-acre field of brush and bramble at my family's country home. This is where my dream of starting my flower business began. Both my daughters were now occupied with school, so I wanted to sink my teeth into a new and exciting project and get re-engaged with the outside world on a professional level. But mostly, I wanted to create a business out of something that I loved.

Years prior, I had left my job in corporate travel to be at home with my two girls while they were very young. These were the best days of my life, and I consider myself fortunate that I was able to do this. When our oldest daughter was ready for kindergarten, we moved onto my husband's family estate property to raise our little family. It's a gorgeous parcel of land in the Santa Cruz Mountains, in a bucolic community called Bonny Doon. Here, we are surrounded by towering coastal redwood and fir trees, which provide an awe-inspiring environment for me and my family. Living in Bonny Doon gives me peace and solace, the antidote to a sometimes-crazy world. We all have that place, or at least we should, that evokes emotions and fosters connections with nature. We become philosophical in these special places of the heart, and Bonny Doon does that for me.

So, for several weeks I kept going back to that spot next to the field of brush and brambles. I decided to plant a garden there and grow lots of flowers. I knew my new business would have to involve flowers. I feel at my best in a garden, with dirt under my nails, and throughout my life I have always been surrounded by gardens and gardeners. My most cherished childhood memories always involve a garden and flowers. Both sets of my grandparents had beautiful gardens, and both of my parents were also avid plant lovers and gardeners, so it's in my genes I suppose!

While I knew that planting a garden and growing lots of flowers was far from a legitimate business plan, I needed to start somewhere. Besides, I think planning and planting a garden is a lot of fun! My desire was to create a business out of something that I love, and I love growing flowers. It satiates my longing to be in nature, and it calibrates my soul. In addition to growing my flowers, I wanted to learn how to create gorgeous floral arrangements, which would satisfy my creative mind. But it was, and still is important to me to work with *real* flowers—which to me are locally farmed and beautifully grown garden flowers. I wanted romantic, fragrant, billowy, and ephemeral flowers, not the stiff and lifeless flowers most florists were using at the time.

Along with my deep love of flowers, I had another passion—and that was the *language* of flowers. I had become captivated with the bygone passion of using flowers to communicate messages during my late teen years. In high school we had Carnation Days, where someone would buy a carnation for another person, with each color containing a different message. Red meant *love*, of course, and we were all eager to see who would receive a red carnation that day. I never received a red carnation, but I'll never forget receiving a pink carnation from a "secret admirer." And after all these years, I still don't know who that carnation came from!

While I sat looking out into this field of brush and brambles, I thought about how astounding it is that by using a floral dictionary, you can communicate highly elaborate messages without saying a word. All sorts of feelings can be portrayed and symbolized by using flowers, plants, trees, and herbs found in gardens, fields, forests, and even patio pots. But not one florist, flower shop, or independent floral designer that I knew of used the language of flowers in their floristry work. Sadly, borrowing sentiments from flowers and plants fell out of popularity over time, but I saw an opportunity to change this by becoming a flower grower and a florist. This new business, I thought, could give me the vehicle I needed to reintroduce the historical language of flowers.

So, on that that afternoon, while sitting out on the edge of that field, my business plan fell into place. I would grow some amazingly beautiful flowers and learn to become a florist. And then, by using and practicing the historical language of flowers to create sentiments, I would try to give the language of flowers a new life and place in our modern world of floristry. This was the birth of my business, Bonny Doon Garden Company, named after the place that inspired me to start a new career in flowers—Bonny Doon, my beloved mountain community that evokes such a tranquil and peaceful way of life to me.

a posy for you

A Lovely Engagement

White Carnation; *Pure & Ardent love*

Lily of the Valley; *You've made my life complete*

Eriostemon; *My beloved*

Maidenhair Fern; *Secret bond of love*

Ivy Geranium; *Bridal favor*

Hazel; *Marriage protection*

Dicentra; *Undying love*

When you look at a floral design, it should make you feel as you're remembering a beautiful garden. A lily should look and smell like it's been just cut from the back-fence line, and a rose should smell like a *rose*. Flowers should evoke emotions, memories, and most of all, adoration for their ephemeral beauty. And when you want to convey a very special message, there is nothing like a posy. And overall, the reaction from a recipient of a posy is what drove me to write this book—I want to pass on that joy, and continue my efforts to rekindle the bygone tradition of floriography, the art of communicating messages with flowers.

WHAT EXACTLY IS A POSY?

By my own definition, a posy is a small flower bouquet—an intimate circular gathering of flowers, plants, and herbs that convey messages in the language of flowers. They're like floral greeting cards. Posies have a very long history, and while trying to uncover the origin of the word posy, I discovered that even in very early times, there was some confusion as to what a posy actually was. A bunch of flowers, and the terms *poesy*, *posy*, *nosegay*, or *bouquet*, were discussed in a *Chicago Daily Tribune* article from April 23, 1892: "posy originally meant verses presented with a nosegay, then came to be applied to the flowers themselves, and finally became the brief poetical sentiment, motto, or legend inscribed upon a ring for the finger." It was during the Victorian Era that the nosegays and posies, rather than the written verse that once accompanied them, began to carry the sentiments in the language of flowers. Today, when we think of a posy, we think of a small, rounded bunch of flowers. For the most part, we have abandoned the notion that they were once used to convey messages.

Nosegays, posies, and tussies have existed since medieval times, where they were carried to ward off disease or evil spirits. During these early times, it was believed that foul odors caused the plague and other illnesses. These posies would have consisted of a few sprigs of fragrant herbs and possibly a flower or two, and were bound by string or twine and placed into pouches to be hung around the neck, waist, or a breast pocket. The term *nosegay* refers to an "ornament for the nose." Nosegays also came in handy to disguise foul odors in the streets of towns and cities prior to public sanitation.

According to the Oxford English Dictionary, the term *tussie-mussie* first appeared in print in 1440: "tyte tust or tusemose of flowyrs or othyr herbys." Moss was used to keep the stems dampened, hence the origin of the name: *tussie*—suggesting a tussock of flowers, or a bunch, and *mussie*—referring to the moss that was used to keep the stems moist. The tussie-mussie became very popular during the reign of Queen Victoria (1837–1901). The tiny bouquets were placed into ornate holders—tussie-mussie holders—and became a popular fashion accessory. They were available in a variety of shapes and designs, usually made of silver, and ladies wore them pinned to a bodice or skirt of a dress or pinned into the hair.

Lily of the valley placed in a bronze tussie-mussie conveys a beautiful sentiment of delicacy, purity, and love's good fortune.

An example of a tussie-mussie holder that includes a finger hole. This was a convenient feature should they need to let go (while dancing!), as it enabled the wearer to release their grip and let the tussie hang from a finger.

Their small size makes them a bit challenging to work with when the goal is to create a modern-day posy that conveys a message using several flowers, plants, and herbs. But I do enjoy using these vintage tussie-mussie holders to create single-flower, or mono-botanical, messages, in this case heather, which means wishes come true.

Here I have used wallpaper to create a tussie-mussie holder. Inside, I've tucked a posy that has been bound with twine, then wrapped in dampened moss. You can also place dampened cotton balls on the bottom of the stems, wrap them in plastic, and then rubber band them.

THE MODERN-DAY POSY

I started creating a modern-day version of a posy after becoming inspired by the many historical language of flowers dictionaries, and beautiful, vintage tussie-mussie holders. The posies that you see in this book are more refined than a traditional tussie-mussie or nosegay. A modern posy is a structured floral design, and is domed in style or, as in French, *pavé*, in a way that is aesthetically pleasing. It is a concisely rounded floral arrangement, rich in textures and balanced in color, and approximately 6 to 8 inches in diameter.

In this book, I will explain how to be resourceful in using beautiful garden flowers; grower bunches from a florist, farmer's market, or grocery store; cuttings from your backyard hedges; herbs from your patio pots; and more to create these little gems that are so full of meaning. They are a nod to our history and they satiate our desire to slow down and admire the beauty our natural world gives us. They also allow us to ponder the beautiful sentiments and meanings behind our abundant collections of flowers, herbs, and plants. Creating a posy is a form of meditation for me, and it can be for you as well. I have found that when you take the time to create a posy—which entails thinking of what sentiments and emotions you want to portray—the process grounds you to into the moment while connecting you to the person you are making the posy for. You are concentrating on flowers, plants, and herbs and their coded messages—their language and that act makes you reflect on your own emotions and thoughts too.

Just look around you. Plants, trees, and flowers are everywhere, and they are ripe with meaning. The hedges of boxwood outside your office mean *stoicism*. The petunias on the patio mean *your presence soothes me*, the camellia on the corner means *beauty* and *excellence*, and that euonymus along the driveway stands for *long life*. There are gifts of messages and sentiments just outside your door, and you'll soon forget all about Facebook, Instagram, and making dinner too! What a wonderful respite from the hectic schedules we try too hard to keep up with. Using the language of flowers today lends its charms to friendship, to gratitude, maternal affection, love, sympathy, and just to say *hello, and I'm thinking of you*.

For all their symbolic meanings, beauty, and fragrance, using flowers to convey messages truly settles itself into our hearts and souls. There are few other gifts that are guaranteed to evoke emotions and set a heart melting. Dinner and a movie? Those are gone in 3 to 4 hours. A gift of a posy will last for 4 to 6 days. And after the ephemeral beauty of the flowers has waned away, the beautiful sentiment tag you attach to the posy can be cherished forever. I'm so happy you're going to make some posies with me, and I hope you find it just as rewarding as I do.

Suna and Inan Kiraç Foundation
Orientalist Paintings Collection

A History of
the Language of Flowers

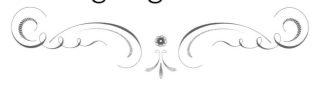

The history of the language of flowers is complex and intricate. It is a controversial subject, and the origin of the language of flowers that we are familiar with today is not entirely clear. There is even some uncertainty about people *ever* using flowers to convey messages to one another. In her book *The Language of Flowers: A History*, Beverly Seaton states that there is virtually no evidence of the practice of exchanging message bouquets in the nineteenth century, which is when the language of flowers phenomenon occurred in England. The invention and development of the language of flowers, she says, was an artistic fabrication that took the form of sentimental flower books, almanacs, and calendars. While this may or may not be true, the fact remains that we continue to be enthralled by the *idea* that we can use flowers to transmit messages, and that floriography can take the place of words when our human nature demands our voices be silent—whether from the deep love we feel for another person or out of quiet respect, a repose when no words can convey the feeling of loss. There is no other object or set of objects that can replace words in such an eloquent and perfect way as beautiful flowers.

The idea of floral symbolism and the language of flowers has been with us for a very, very long time and that is all we really need to understand. It's up to us whether we continue to recognize and honor and apply this tradition.

Throughout much of human history, flowers have symbolized all sorts of milestones, sentiments, superstitions, religious beliefs, passions, and afflictions. Hieroglyphics of ancient Egypt formed the earliest written language of flowers, with pictures that tell stories using plants and animals. Before written language was perfected, ancient cultures used flowers, plants, and animals to convey their thoughts and tell their stories. Remains of roses have been found in Egyptian tombs, and a red rose is pictured at the four-thousand-year-old Palace of Knossos on the island of Crete. To this day, the rose continues to be a symbol of love and purity.

We have adorned ourselves with their beauty and representations for ceremonies, used flowers for badges for our heroes, and looked to them for representation of seasons, months, and years. We have long used flowers to commemorate milestones in our lives, to honor marriages, and mourn death. We celebrate with flowers, we decorate with flowers. There is simply nothing in our natural world that captivates more than a flower. They are visually stunning and their fragrance can be so intense and clear we can almost taste it. They beckon us with their transient beauty, and we become captivated by their flawless structure and intoxicating fragrances. Flowers and the roles they play in our lives are simply indispensable.

FROM SÉLAM TO PHENOMENON

The language of flowers that we are familiar with today is said to have been inspired by the early Turkish *sélam*. During Ottoman times, a *sélam* was a greeting of objects. A box of objects (or objects wrapped in cloth handkerchiefs) was gifted from one to another, and each object carried a rhyme, which, once translated and pondered, held a meaning. According to Beverly Seaton's *The Language of Flowers: A History*, the objects themselves weren't symbolic of any one meaning, but their meaning rhymed with the object's name. For example, *armoude* (pear) is not given a meaning for what ideas it might suggest, but for words that rhyme with its name, such as *omoude* (hope). The sélam was not like the language of flowers as we understand it today, nor a secret language of lovers, but it did give the idea of a language of love conveyed by objects rather than words.

In an essay regarding the language of objects and the origin of the sélam, Austrian historian and orientalist Joseph von Hammer-Purgstall (1774–1856) wrote that the sélam was "merely a harem game, an amusement by the women of the harem to pass the time." It remains uncertain why or how the language of objects, or how the custom of the sélam, was developed. But, since there was no communication allowed between the women of the harem and the outside world, it would make sense that one might devise this clever tactic to overcome the harem's boundaries, and slip hidden messages to an outsider, or just to pass her time in a creative and inventive way.

In modern-day Turkey, a *sélam* is still a greeting, and a way of saying hello. It also means to have a good day, and peace, as in "I come in peace," which ties in with the Arabic translation of *salam*, "peace." There is also a religious form of the *sélam* greeting, but this use has been dropped in the past hundred years or so, and today the *sélam* is a secular way of greeting someone, but still more formal than just a casual "hi."

The Lady Mary Wortley Montagu, wife of John Montagu, the English ambassador to Turkey, resided in Constantinople from 1716–18. During which time she was able to gain access to Ottoman society, and in particular to socialize with Ottoman women. The Lady Mary was charmed by the custom of the sélam among the women, and upon her return to England she wrote about this custom in her society letters. The letters became very popular in England and were known as the "Turkish Embassy Letters," and they were published posthumously under the same title in 1763. Through symbols and meanings of objects, she wrote, "you can either quarrel, reproach, or send letters of passion, friendship, or civility, or even news, without even inking your fingers. There is no flower, no fruit, herb nor feather, that has not a verse belonging to it." These letters were at least partly responsible for generating the phenomenon of the language of flowers in England during the nineteenth century.

The sélam was romanticized by westerners where they created their own version of a sélam, a gifting of objects, using flowers, plants, and herbs, and forgoing the rhyme and giving symbolic meaning to them. The Victorian-era British, who were coming out of a twenty-year war with France, were understandably ready for romance and sentimentalism. What began as a greeting of objects in the Ottoman Empire, became the first signs of western floriography of the early nineteenth century. Subsequently, there were many developments and publications of miniature and finely illustrated gift books depicting floral dictionaries and symbolism. The popular concept of gift books had spawned an onslaught of flower dictionaries.

One of the earliest language of flowers books was French, published in 1810, by B. Delachénaye. In his introduction to his floral dictionary, he argues that a real sélam contained only flowers. Well, here we are again with a differing statement of how it all began! The most prevalent of the early dictionaries was *Le language des fleurs*, published in 1819 and written by Charlotte de la Latour (the pen name of Louise Cortambert). This book could be found on the drawing room tables of virtually every French genteel woman.

By far the most popular for the English language of flowers books was Frederic Shoberl, Louise Cortambert, and Louis-Aimé Martin's *The language of flowers: with illustrative poetry,* published in 1848. The flower as a "messenger of the heart" had certainly become hugely popular in the nineteenth century. During the reign of Queen Victoria many floral dictionaries were published, including a very comprehensive meaning of flowers in John Ingram's *Flora Symbolica, or The language and sentiment of flowers. Including floral poetry, original and selected.*

In the United States, the first books on floriography were Elizabeth Wirt's *Flora's Dictionary* and Dorothea Dix's *The Garland of Flora*, both of which were published in 1829. During its peak in America, the language of flowers attracted the attention of the most popular women writers and editors of the day. Language of flowers poems and writings were featured in poplar magazines and many gift books with beautiful illustrations and floral symbolism were published during this time. My personal favorite is *Flora's Lexicon*, written by Catharine H. Waterman and published in 1855. I have used this book as reference and continue to enjoy her poem "The Language of Flowers" as inspiration and often reflect on its intricate dance in words:

> Yes–flowers have tones–God gave to each
> A language of its own,
> And bade the simple blossom teach
> Where'er its seeds are sown

Today there are still language of flowers books being published, but there are few compared to the prolific eighteenth century. Happily, we have not lost touch with the historical art of floriography, and we will continue, I am certain, to be enthralled with nature's awe-inspiring gift to us—a language of flowers.

IN EASTERN LANDS

In China, Korea, and Japan, flowers have also held myth and meaning since ancient times. Plum blossoms, orchid, bamboo, and chrysanthemums have long been featured in paintings and poems to express loftiness, righteousness, modesty, and purity. Because they symbolize these human virtues, they are known as "the four gentlemen."

In ancient China, flowers were grown and harvested for their symbolic meaning. The peony, which has been cultivated throughout Asia for centuries, remains the most honored flower, symbolizing wealth, prosperity, status, and fortune. Considered to be the unofficial Chinese National Flower, the peony is used throughout China in many celebrations and is favored as a wedding anniversary flower. The plants require much diligence and meticulous care in growing, hence two of their meanings of wealth and prosperity, because only the wealthiest could afford this sort of high-maintenance cultivation. It is also symbolic of spring, female beauty, and reproduction.

In Chinese culture, the lotus is the most precious and symbolic flower, as it represents the holy seat of Buddha. The lotus flower rises from the mud and blooms in beauty, symbolizing perfection and purity of both the heart and

Lady Mary Wortley Montagu, 1689–1762

In addition to her successful poetry, Lady Wortley Montagu achieved other great feats. Notably, her writings addressing and challenging the social injustices toward women, as well as her distinguished success in introducing and advocating for smallpox inoculation to western medicine after her return from Turkey. She was a respectable advocate ahead of her time and brought to light problems in the best way she knew how—through writing and poetry. "I sometimes give myself admirable advice, but I am incapable of taking it," she wrote.

An excerpt from Frederic Shoberl, Louise Cortambert, and Louis-Aimé Martin's 1848 book *The language of flowers: with illustrative poetry*, which exemplifies the romantic expression on the sélam:

Castellan, in his "Letter on Greece," mentions that when he was passing through the lovely valley of Bujukdern on the Bosphorus, his attention was attracted by a little country pleasure-house, surrounded by a neat garden. Beneath one of the grated windows stood a young Turk, who after playing a light prelude on the tambur, a sort of mandoline, sang a love-song, in which the following verse occurred:

The nightingale wander from flower to flower, seeking the rose, his heart's only prize;

Thus, did my love change every hour, Until I saw thee, light of my eyes!

No sooner was the song ended than a small white hand opened the lattice of the window and dropped a bunch of flowers. The young Turk picked up the nosegay and appeared to read in some secret message. He pressed it to his bosom, then fastened it in his turban, and after making some signs towards the window, he withdrew. The young gallant appeared from his dress to be nothing more than a poor water-carrier. But the Turkish proverb says that, however high a woman may rear her head towards the clouds, her feet nevertheless touch the earth. The girl was actually the daughter of a rich Jew, worth a hundred thousand piastres.

mind. It also stands for long life and honor. The lotus flower has been depicted in Chinese art, poetry, and architecture throughout a long history, and into modern times.

There is also crossover between Eastern and Western flower meanings and symbolism. The chrysanthemum in China is a good example. Drawing on its meanings of cheerfulness and optimism in our Western dictionaries, I use the chrysanthemum in birthday posies in a celebratory way. In China, these flowers symbolize a strong life force and are often given to the elderly for this reason. They can also represent good luck to the home and a life of comfort. White chrysanthemums stand for nobility and elegance, just as in the United States, and are used as offerings at spiritual shrines. In China, other than the white chrysanthemum available for use in shrines, white flowers are not used because of their representation of death and ghosts.

Some flowers with positive meanings in the West have negative ones in China. For example, in the West spring flowering branches stand for rebirth and the beauty of spring, while in Chinese culture they stand for an unfaithful lover, as the petals are easily scattered. And in China, any flower that blooms on a thorny branch represents pain and unhappiness, so there goes the coveted rose and all its multileveled meanings in the Western language of flowers!

Hanakotoba refers to the ancient art of assigning meanings to flowers in Japan. In Japanese culture, flowers and their meanings are of great importance and can be used to communicate emotions without using words, so giving flowers to another is not taken lightly. Like western floriography, hanakotoba has fallen out of popularity in modern times, however, it is still used in the Japanese floral design practice of ikebana. Flowers and plants are arranged in a very special way in ikebana, to represent three points: earth, moon, and sun, or alternately, sun or man, earth, and heaven. In addition to these representations, the meanings of flowers are also considered in order to reflect a certain message for the recipient or observer.

Flowers are used for ceremonies in Japan, just as they are in the West, but there are certain customs that are endemic to Japan. For example, a *chabana* is a special presentation of flowers for a ceremonial tea that includes branches and twigs from the surrounding area, along with seasonal blooms, and is often displayed in a bamboo vase. The chabana is thought to establish a connection with nature and connect the ceremonial tearoom to the surrounding land. A *kadomatsu* is a floral arrangement made from bamboo and pine, then placed outside the door to celebrate the coming of the New Year. It is used to welcome the gods to the home and believed to promote health and happiness during the upcoming year.

The cherry blossom is a symbol of nationalism in Japan. In the days of the Samurais, it was a depiction of how fleeting their life could be. The Samurai had always been guided by their knowledge and understanding that they should live their life brilliantly however brief it may be, and go down dramatically, just as the cherry blossoms look gloriously magnificent when in full bloom, only to fall to the ground after a short while. Cherry blossoms are associated with the concept of *mono no aware*, a Japanese phrase that could be translated to "feelings for the passing of things." The overall principle of *mono no aware* is that we should recognize the impermanence of life, and of everything that exists, and create a deeper connection with it because of its fleeting nature. In other words, enjoy every moment of your life, and understand that change and brevity are essential to earthly existence.

And as beautiful as they are, camellias can be considered bad luck in Japan due to one of the flower's characteristics: Instead of the petals falling one by one, the entire head of the flower falls off the stem. I suppose it is a little disturbing when you look under your camellia tree and see all the flower heads lying lifelessly on the ground. It makes perfect sense that this could seem like a curse of bad luck!

For the Japanese, just as in many other cultures, flowers are used to differentiate the *types* of love, not just a singular passionate love. Some of the meanings are the same as the Western definitions, but there are some differences:

- Rose: Like Victorian and other Western interpretations, the red rose represents romantic love in Japanese culture, but as in Western culture, it is not the only flower that represents love.

- Red Japanese Lotus: The red lotus stands for love, passion, and compassion.

- Forget-Me-Not: Delicate blue forget-me-nots represent true love.

- Red Camelia: The red camelia represents being *in love*.

- Gardenia: Gardenias symbolize a crush or secret love.

- Tulip: The tulip represents one-sided or unrequited love.

- Carnation: The carnation stands for passion.

- Cactus: A cactus flower symbolizes lust (or sex).

In the far East, the West, and everywhere in between, virtually all civilizations and cultures throughout history have used flowers and plants to symbolize beliefs and play roles in rituals, as well as to communicate messages. Imagine now, when you are making a posy, that you are taking part in a ritual as old as civilization—as long as we've existed!

Posy Recipes

There are infinite possibilities when combining flowers, herbs, and plants to create an overall sentiment or message in a posy. In this section you will find posy recipes for some common messages such as *Happy Birthday* as well as for unique and fun sentiments such as *Glamour Girl*. Use these recipes as they are, or with some of the alternate ingredients listed with them, depending upon what flowers and herbs you have available. I have noted their seasonal availability in the garden, but you may be able to obtain some more popular flowers year-round from various outlets as listed in the Resource Directory (page 241). I've also noted how many stems to use for each ingredient—just remember that these are approximate. Use more, or less, depending upon individual bloom sizes and the overall desired size of your posy. Let these posy recipes also be a visual cue to prompt your creativity for your *own* personalized sentiment tags that go with the posies! To learn how to prep the flowers and assemble your posy, see page 123.

The Posies

FRIENDS TO THE END

Here is a good example of a truly garden-inspired posy. All these ingredients were selected from readily available garden flowers. The simplicity and familiarity of the ingredients in this posy create a charming presentation that almost everyone relates to. The combination of carefully chosen harmonious colors and complementary textures makes it hard to beat a gift like this.

Ingredients used are available in the summer and early fall garden

5–7 stems Pink Carnation: *women's love*

5–6 stems Oak-leaf Geranium: *true friends*

7–10 stems Euphorbia: *protection*

8–10 stems Mint: *warmth of feeling*

3–5 stems Alstromeria: *friendship*

3–5 stems Peach-color Rose: *appreciation*

ALTERNATE INGREDIENTS AND SEASONAL VARIATIONS:

Almond Tree (spring, summer): *abiding love & friendship*

Boronia (spring, early summer): *sweetness*

Galax (spring, summer, fall): *friendship*

Siskiyou Pinks (Gaura) (summer): *exhilarating, refreshing personality, ability, intellect*

Mullein (spring, summer, fall): *good nature*

Orchid (year-round greenhouse): *love, thoughtfulness, rare beauty*

Pear Blossoms (spring): *lasting friendship*

Let the sentiment tag be your creative outlet! The recipient will forever cherish a beautifully embellished sentiment tag. The black and white toile scrapbooking paper used here is just the right weight to create tags because it is not too heavy, but can carry some embellishment weight, and hold up to a ribbon strung through it.

Peach Rose

Pink Carnation

Euphorbia

Mint

Alstromeria

Oak-leaf Geranium

BIRTHDAY WISHES

When I give this posy to family or friends, they say it's the best birthday gift they've ever received. I think it's partly because its color and textures are so rich and earthy, but also because the hens and chicks and hardy geranium can be rooted and made into keepsake plants for their own garden. I sent this posy to my mom in Texas, and when the blooms of the callas and cosmos finally faded enough to call them dead, she tossed those, but rooted the geranium and hens and chicks—it is a gift that keeps giving, literally!

And who doesn't fall in love at once with the chocolate cosmo? Its rich deep color summons the eye, and the velvety texture is simply irresistible. Once you take a whiff of a chocolate cosmo you are forever hooked! They really do smell identical to chocolate!

⇒ Ingredients used are available in the spring and summer garden ⇐

7–9 stems Calla Lily: *magnificent beauty*

3–5 stems Hens & Chicks: *long life*

6–9 stems Hardy Geranium: *wishes come true*

12–15 stems Lavender: *luck, success, happiness*

6–9 stems Basil: *best wishes*

5–7 stems Chocolate Cosmos: *simple pleasures*

ALTERNATE INGREDIENTS AND SEASONAL VARIATIONS:

Stock (summer): *lasting beauty*

Lemon Balm (spring, summer, fall): *fun*

Chrysanthemum (fall): *cheerfulness, long life*

White Cosmos (summer): *joy in love and life*

Coral Rose (summer, fall): *longevity*

Oregano (summer): *joy, happiness*

DESIGN TIP:

Some flowers and plants are more difficult than others to use in posies because of their shape, stem thickness, and the way the flower is constructed. One of these is the calla lily. I love using the calla because its sentiment lends itself to many occasions. But, they are difficult to work into a posy and maintain a nice overall domed or pavé shape. Because the calla is chalice-shaped, it will always protrude in one way or another. The easiest, quickest way to solve that is to determine which way the calla naturally wants to lay, and then try to point the tip toward the outer side of the posy rather than pointing inward.

Chocolate Cosmo

Hens & Chicks (Sempervivum)

Lavender

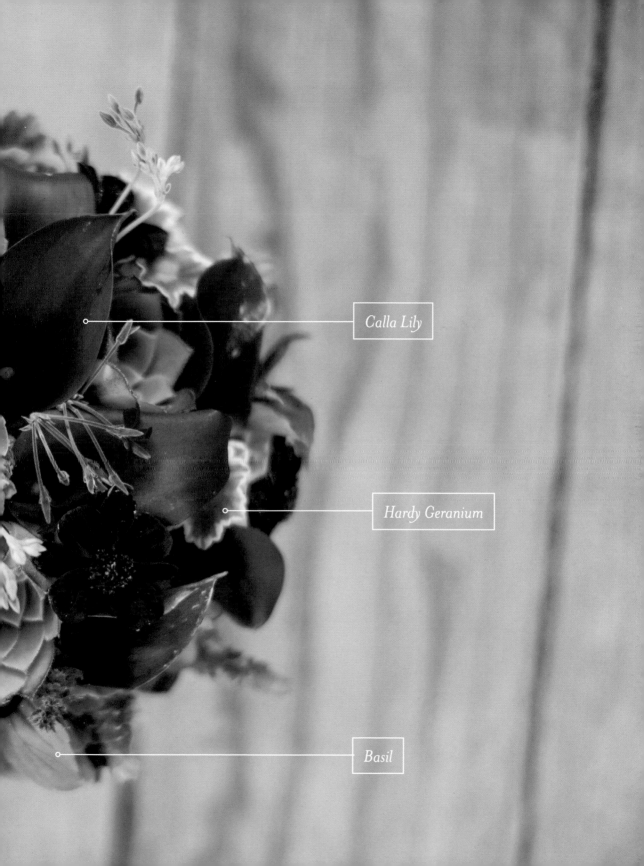

Calla Lily

Hardy Geranium

Basil

THE GLAMOUR GIRL POSY

Glamour Girl is for the lady who can walk the walk and talk the talk! When you need to celebrate your lady friends' awesomeness, for whatever reason—birthday, girlfriends' day, or just because you want her to know she's awesome and you love her—if there is a perfect "girlfriend" posy, this is it! What an amazing show of love, admiration, and girl power.

Ingredients used are available in the summer garden

3–5 stems Coleus: *excitement, energy, showy*

3–5 stems Lisianthus: *kind thoughts*

6–8 stems White Geranium: *gracefulness*

7–10 stems Deutzia: *delicate and ample beauty*

7–9 stems Horehound: *virtue, fire*

1 Fully-blown Rose: *beauty at its finest*

ALTERNATE INGREDIENTS AND SEASONAL VARIATIONS:

Abutilon (summer): *grace, dignity*

Acacia Rose (spring, summer): *elegance*

Alder (spring, summer, fall): *symbol of glamour*

California Poppy (summer): *sweetness*

Gaura (summer): *exhilarating, refreshing personality, ability, intellect*

Crepe Myrtle (spring, early summer): *eloquence*

NOTE:
When the delicate petals of a rose are fully laid open to feel the warm kiss of the sun, they release their exquisite fragrance. Only when a rose is fully open like this can you enjoy its extraordinary perfume and see its intricate layered pattern of petals. A fully-opened rose, especially a damask or other heirloom garden rose, truly is an example of beauty at its finest.

Here is an opportunity to have some fun with your sentiment tag. Since your posy's sentiments are fun and glamorous, you can jazz up the tag accordingly!

Fully-blown Rose

Horehound

Lisianthus

White Geranium

Coleous

Deutzia

THE QUEEN FOR A DAY POSY

Along the same lines as The Glamour Girl, this is another good posy for a friend who is celebrating a birthday or just needs to feel like a queen for a day or more!

→ Ingredients used are available in the spring and summer garden ←

5–7 stems Calla Lily: *magnificent beauty*

3 stems Camellia: *excellence*

5–7 stems Cestrum: *transient beauty*

3 stems Gardenia: *feminine charm*

3–5 stems Magnolia: *splendid beauty*

7–9 stems Sweet Marjoram: *kindness*

ALTERNATE INGREDIENTS AND SEASONAL VARIATIONS:

Canna (summer, fall): *magnificent beauty*

Alder (spring, summer, fall): *glamour*

Clematis (summer, fall): *mental beauty*

Crepe Myrtle (late spring, early summer): *eloquence*

Peppermint Geranium (summer, fall): *inspiration*

Hoya (summer): *pure loveliness*

DESIGN TIP:
This posy has some of the most challenging materials to work with because of the various shapes and sizes. The calla, being chalice-shaped, has to be worked into the arrangement in a way that it "lays" facing outward, so there are no protrusions of its elegant, pointed tip. The gardenia, being flat-faced, needs to be placed in such a way that it shows its "face" at pleasing angles. And finally, the camellia stems are rigid and hard, and the bloom itself is rarely upward facing. I have found that wiring the gardenia and camellia blooms and taping their stems will make it easier to place these blooms in a posy at a pleasing angle (see page 136 for instructions).

Calla Lily

Camellia

Sweet Marjoram

Magnolia

Gardenia

Cestrum

Happy 50ᵗʰ Dear Sister!

Amaryllis: *splendid beauty*
Cream Rose: *perfection, richness*
Rue: *grace*
Ranunculus: *radiant with charm*
Fritillaria: *pride of birth, majesty*
Amaranth: *everlasting friendship*
Hellebore: *a beautiful year ahead*
Bassia: *resilient, adaptable*
Silver-leaf Geranium: *admiration*

A SPECIAL BIRTHDAY!

This is a splendid posy to celebrate a milestone birthday and is an excellent example of the richness and beauty of what a well-thought-out gift of a posy can be. It's creative, gorgeous, and packed with wonderful sentiments.

   This posy will be so well-received and never forgotten—it saturates the senses with such heartfelt and expressive messages, it will surely be the icing on the cake!

Ingredients used are available in the spring and summer garden

9–12 stems Cream-color Rose: *perfection, richness*

5–9 stems Bassia: *resilient, adaptable*

3–5 stems Hellebore: *a beautiful year ahead*

5–9 stems Ranunculus: *radiant with charm*

1 stem Amaryllis: *splendid beauty*

9–12 stems Silver-leaf Geranium: *admiration*

5–7 stems Amaranth: *everlasting friendship*

3 stems Fritillaria: *pride of birth, majesty*

7–9 stems Rue: *grace*

ALTERNATE INGREDIENTS AND SEASONAL VARIATIONS:

Russian Sage (summer): *knowledge and wisdom*

Smoke Bush (spring): *radiant and dreamy*

Wallflower (summer): *lasting beauty*

Astrantia (summer, fall): *strength, power, courage, protection*

Salad Burnet (spring, summer, fall): *a merry heart*

Camellia (late winter, spring): *beauty, excellence, loveliness*

NOTE:
I love using hellebore in any sort of celebratory or best-wishes posy because of the sentiment. The blooms can be used for a long period of time—during the late winter and spring when they're in the bloom season, and long into summer and early fall by leaving the bloom on the plant to age. They will usually turn a beautiful light to medium green color, which looks beautiful with almost any color palette.

There are nine ingredients in this posy, which is more than what goes into the average posy. So, there's a lot of texture and color packed into this small-sized posy! When selecting a larger number of ingredients to use, be sure to keep in mind the color palette, and the plants' textures and shapes, and try not to use too much of any one ingredient. This is the key in making it look harmonious and elegant. The colors in this posy are complementary to one another and mostly analogous, while the textures aren't too harsh, with the silver-leafed geranium and ranunculus softening things up. I love using a larger number of ingredients, especially when it turns out like this!

Amaryllis

Rue

Fritillaria

Amaranth

Silver-leafed Geranium

Bassia

Cream Rose

Hellebores

Ranunculus

WELCOME BABY GIRL POSY

What a glorious way to welcome a baby girl to the world! The colors and textures here are so elegant, with sentiments fitting a sweet little lady-to-be. A bundle of delicate and precious joy! Wishes and hopes for an enchanted lifetime full of beauty, delicate pleasures, happiness, and unfading love are the things we want for our newborns. This posy matches those wishes and hopes, with delicate colors and diverse textures that are so well-balanced you won't want to give this posy away—but you'll be so happy you did! Another nice thing about this posy is that the roses and herbs can be dried and made into a lovely potpourri or sachet for long-term enjoyment.

Ingredients used are available in the summer garden

7–12 stems Globe Amaranth: *unfading love*

5–9 stems Acacia Leaves: *my heart is buried with affection*

5–7 stems Japanese Maple: *baby's hands*

6–9 stems Lavender Rose: *enchantment*

1–3 stems Hydrangea: *haven, protection*

8–12 stems Lavender: *happiness*

7–19 stems Caryopteris: *delightful presence*

7–9 stems Sweet Pea: *delicate pleasures*

ALTERNATE INGREDIENTS AND SEASONAL VARIATIONS:

Caladium (summer): *great joy*

Oregano (spring, summer, fall): *happiness*

Hypericum (summer, fall): *protection*

Blue Iris (spring): *faith, hope, wisdom*

Purple-leaf Sage (spring, summer, fall): *gratitude*

Violet (late winter, spring): *sweet beauty*

Welcome Baby Girl!

Caryopteris Pagoda; delightful
presence
Sweet Pea; delicate pleasures
Japanese Maple; baby's hands
Lavender Rose; enchantment
Hydrangea; haven, protection
Globe Amaranth; unfading love
Lavender; happiness
Rose Acacia; elegance

Sweet Pea

Caryopteris

Globe Amaranth

Lavender

Acacia leaves

Lavender Rose

Japanese Maple

Hydrangea

a posy for you

Welcome Baby Boy!

Borage; *Courage*
White Sage; *Protection,
Health*
Hydrangea; *Luck, Success,
Happiness*
Cerinthe; *Enduring, Timeless
affection*
Blue Salvia; *Wisdom*
Japanese Maple; *Baby's
Hands*
Blueberry; *Prayer, Protection*
Arborvitae; *Tree of life*

WELCOME BABY BOY POSY

Oh boy! Talk about textures! Here, beautiful greens with pops of varied hues of blues and purples set off an elegant feel. This is such a rich and elegant posy. And look at the blueberries! It's not often we get to use blueberries in floral design, so making a posy using some of the more uncommon flower-arranging ingredients is a nice change of pace. What a perfectly stunning and fun gift for a new mom welcoming a bouncing baby boy into the world.

→ Ingredients used are available in the summer garden ←

3–5 stems Blue Salvia: *wisdom*

7–9 stems Cerinthe: *enduring, timeless affection*

1 stem Hydrangea: *luck, success, happiness*

3–4 stems White Sage: *protection, health*

1–3 stems Blueberry: *prayer, protection*

5–7 stems Japanese Maple: *baby's hands*

3–5 stems Borage: *courage*

5 stems Arborvitae: *tree of life*

DESIGN TIP:
Using a base of hydrangea is very helpful when including heavy ingredients such as a stem of blueberries. The umbel-shape of the hydrangea can serve as a base to stick the heavy stems in. It's also a great filling material and gives needed volume when you're using several leafy greens and herbs.

ALTERNATE INGREDIENTS AND SEASONAL VARIATIONS:

Hopseed Bush (spring, summer, fall): *abundance in creativity, impervious to adversity*

Iris (spring): *faith, wisdom, valor*

Ixia (spring): *happiness*

Jade (year-round): *health and happiness*

Juniper (year-round): *protection*

Arborvitae

Borage

Blueberry

Japanese Maple

Blue Salvia

Cerinthe

Hydrangea

White Sage

THE HOUSE WARMING POSY

There are many opportunities in our lives to give this posy because it stands for hospitality, joy, and friendship. A gift of a House Warming Posy to a new neighbor, friend, or relative who has just moved into a new home will never be forgotten. I also love leaving this posy in the guest room for our houseguests. It says *welcome to our home* like nothing else can.

The look and feel of this posy isn't showy or extravagant, but rather modest and familiar. Using materials from the garden—oak, euphorbia, lavender, scented geranium, and Jerusalem sage—lends an extra feel of thoughtfulness to this arrangement. Its rich texture and subtle colors blend well into all environments and the sentiments are so heartfelt and suitable the recipient will surely cherish this gift.

Ingredients used are available in the spring, summer, and fall garden

7–12 stems Jerusalem Sage: *pride of ownership*
8–10 stems Broom: *safety*
3–7 stems Oak: *hospitality*
7–9 stems Eurphorbia: *welcome*
15 stems Lavender: *luck, happiness*
7–12 stems Scented Geranium: *comfort, gentility*

DESIGN TIP:
Jerusalem sage is an indeterminate line flower, which means it must be *topped-off* (for instructions see page 135) to use in a posy. Since the florets are positioned going up the stem and get smaller as it climbs, you need to cut off the top portions of the stem and use the first prominent bloom in the posy.

ALTERNATE INGREDIENTS AND SEASONAL VARIATIONS:
Comfrey (summer): *home sweet home*
Wood Sorrel (spring, summer, fall): *joy*
Pineapple Sage (spring, summer, fall): *hospitality, happy home*
White Sage (spring, summer, fall): *purification of space*
Safflower (fall): *welcome*
Yellow Rose (summer, fall): *congratulations, friendship*
Sage (spring, summer, fall): *domestic virtue*
Juniper (year-round): *protection, welcome to new home*

a p... for you

HOUSE WARMING

Oak; hospitality
Lavender; luck, happiness
Broom; safety
Euphorbia; welcome
Jerusalem Sage; pride of
ownership
Scented Geranium; comfort,
gentility

Jerusalem Sage

Lavender

Euphorbia

Broom

Scented Geranium

Oak

a posy for you

Welcome Home!
Sedum; welcome, tranquility
Berzelia; humility, admiration
Rose; love, beauty, friendship
Astrantia; strength, power, courage, protection
Stock; lasting beauty
Lavender; luck, success, happiness
Everlasting; never-ceasing remembrance
Pelargonium; true friend

WELCOME HOME

When someone has been gone and you're ready to welcome them back, this posy will make them feel like they need to go away more often so they can come back to this! A very memorable and beautiful posy that conveys sentiments of tranquility, beauty, comfort, love, and friendship will make them feel special and welcomed.

Ingredients used are available in the spring, summer, and fall garden

3–5 stems Sedum: *welcome, tranquility*

5–7 stems Berzelia: *humility, admiration*

5–7 stems Roses: *love, beauty, friendship*

7–9 stems Astrantia: *strength, power, courage, protection*

3–5 stems Stock: *lasting beauty*

9–11 stems Lavender: *luck, success, happiness*

5–7 stems Everlasting: *never-ceasing remembrance*

3–5 stems Pelargonium: *true friend*

ALTERNATE INGREDIENTS AND SEASONAL VARIATIONS:

American Elm (spring, summer, fall): *patriotism, protection, vigor*

Sage (year-round): *domestic virtue*

Bellflower (summer): *return of a friend is desired*

Cactus (year-round): *bravery, endurance*

Chrysanthemum, bronze-color (fall): *happy hearth and home*

Hydrangea, shrub (spring, summer, fall): *devotion to a noble cause or love, unveiling*

Pelargonium

Everlasting

Rose

Berzelia

Lavender

Sedum

Stock

Astrantia

A LOVELY ENGAGEMENT

There is something purely magical about an engagement to be married. Two people coming together as one, and a promise of a commitment to one another, both filled with hopes, dreams, and pure excitement at what the future holds. This makes everyone giddy with happiness! Here is a beautiful posy that's perfect for congratulations on an engagement. Creating a posy to celebrate this is always such an honor. You can use some of the most romantic and heartfelt sentiments that exist in the language of flowers to create a unique and powerful statement with an engagement posy.

Showing commitment, happiness, and desire to please, the ingredients in this posy are easy to come by in a standard garden, with a little boost from some hybrid roses and gardenia bought at a flower shop.

Ingredients used are available in the spring and summer garden

9–12 stems Maidenhair Fern: *secret bond of love*

5–7 stems Ivy Geranium: *bridal favor*

5–7 stems White Carnation: *pure and ardent love*

5 stems Dicentra: *undying love*

5–7 stems Eriostemon: *my beloved*

5 stems Lily of the Valley: *you've made my life complete*

5–7 stems Hazel: *marriage protection*

Since a large majority of the sentiments in the language of flowers dictionaries that were developed during the romantic era were expressly designed to portray sentiments of love, or the pursuit of love, the choices for alternate materials are extensive. Let the color palette, the sentiments that speak to you, and the desired aesthetic of your posy be your guide.

Hazel

Lily of the Valley

Dicentra

Eriostemon

Maidenhair Fern

Ivy Geranium

White Carnation

Lily of the Valley—if you are fortunate enough to have these in your garden then there is no better flower you can use to commemorate luck, love, and happiness in marriage. And hazel, which offers marriage protection, is often found growing wild on the roadsides and can easily be formed and worked into the posy to lend a nice soft texture and deepen the effect, since the maidenhair fern is so very light and delicate. And what's not to love about the bleeding hearts? And the aroma of this posy is so wonderfully seductive it makes you want to lay down inside it!

a posy for you

Sweet Heart

Eriostemon: my beloved, dear to the
Daphne: desire to please
Carnation: bonds of affection
Ranunculus: charming, attraction
Pink rose: loveliness, grace
Oregano: kindness, happiness
Freesia: humble, love

THE SWEET HEART POSY

This dainty little sweet thing is one of our most popular posies at the flower shop. There is nothing not to love! It can be either given to a daughter or a lover. Every sentiment in this posy is appropriate to show you love and care for someone. Because there are so many definitions in the language of flowers that would be proper to use in a Sweet Heart Posy, the color palette options are expansive, making this posy one of the most accessible and easy to make.

→ Ingredients used are from the spring and summer garden ←

9–12 stems Pink Rose: *beauty, grace*

5–7 stems Fuschia: *humble love*

8–10 stems Eriostemon: *my beloved, dear to me*

5–9 stems Ranunculus: *attraction, charming, you are rich in attractions, I am dazzled by your charms, pride*

7–10 stems Oregano: *kindness, happiness*

5–7 stems Carnation: *bonds of love, affection*

3–5 stems Daphne: *desire to please*

There are many variations you can use to make a Sweet Heart Posy. You can use red roses or red carnations to elevate it to a romantic and passionate love. Or, omit "attraction" in the ranunculus definition, and use only the "charming" part, making it fitting for an innocent, pure love for a daughter, niece, or sister. This is a good example of how flexible the meanings of flowers can be. If you want your posy to be more romantic and show passionate love, then choose from the definitions of each ingredient to portray that feeling and drop other meanings that may be not conducive to your message.

Eriostemon

Ranunculus

Fuscia

Oregano

Carnation

Daphne

Pink Rose

SIMPLEMENT L'AMOUR

The posy nearest and dearest to my heart, *Simplement l'Amour*, is made up of glorious colors and tiny, delicate blooms, flanked by layers of fragrant herbs. This posy is truly a piece of art, and I have enjoyed making many of these through my years of creating posies. This is our most popular posy at the flower shop, because—well, just look at it! The combinations of the play on textures, light and playful and then darker and heavier, creates a perfect balance, and the colors dance between mono- and duo-chromatic, making this posy feel harmonious and rich.

And the sentiments . . . could this posy be any more captivating? It is perfect for an anniversary, Valentine's Day, an engagement, or even a birthday gift for the one you love. What an absolute delight both to be the giver and the receiver of this beauty.

Ingredients used are available in the spring, summer, and early fall garden

12–14 stems Thyme: *bravery*

5–7 stems Rose: *love, beauty*

8–10 stems Ranunculus: *attraction, charming, you are rich in attraction, I am dazzled by your charms, pride*

5–7 stems Scented Geranium: *gentility*

12–14 stems Oregano: *joy, happiness*

7–9 stems Sweet Pea: *delicate pleasures*

7–9 stems Heather: *admiration*

9–12 stems Myrtle: *love, passion*

ALTERNATE INGREDIENTS AND SEASONAL VARIATIONS:

Calla Lily (spring, summer): *magnificent beauty*

Cluster of Musk Roses (summer): *charming*

Heliotrope (summer): *devotion*

Gardenia (summer, or year-round greenhouse): *transport of joy, ecstasy*

American Linden (spring, summer, fall): *marital virtues, conjugal love and matrimony*

Lilac (spring): *beauty, love*

Rose

Sweet Pea

Heather

Myrtle

Oregano

Thyme

Ranunculus

A POSY FOR YO[U]

Congratulations!
Laurel: glory, personal
achievement
Camellia: excellence
Basil: best wishes
Yellow Rose:
congratulations
Lavender: luck, success
Dusty Miller: felicity

THE CONGRATULATIONS POSY

There are so many flowers and herbs appropriate for congratulations that sometimes it's difficult to choose what to use. The standard I always go to is the yellow rose because it signifies congratulations, and it stands for friendship as well as the highest mark of distinction. For this version of the posy I opted to use the camelia because it was in bloom during the time of this spring photoshoot! And that is a great example of what you should do—look around and see what you've got in bloom or what looks particularly robust in your yard and then base the other colors and textures of your posy on that.

Ingredients used are available in the spring and summer garden

4–5 stems Camellia: *excellence*

5–7 stems Laurel: *glory, personal achievement*

5–7 stems Basil: *best wishes*

6–7 stems Yellow Rose: *congratulations*

12 stems Lavender (with leaves): *luck, success*

5–7 stems Dusty Miller: *felicity*

ALTERNATE INGREDIENTS AND SEASONAL VARIATIONS:

Angelica (summer): *inspiration*

Masterwort (spring, summer, fall): *strength, power, courage, protection*

Baby's Breath (summer, fall): *festivity*

Sweet Bay (year-round): *personal achievement, success*

Birch (summer, fall): *new beginnings*

DESIGN TIP:
In this posy, I have used both the bloom and the leaves of the lavender. Leaves are a wonderful way to add fullness and/or color and texture to your posy.

Dusty Miller

Yellow Rose

Lavender

Bay Laurel

Lavender foliage

Camellia

Basil

BEING THANKFUL

The Being Thankful Posy is a versatile statement that can be used for many occasions when you want to reach out with friendship, gratitude, or forgiveness. It's perfect on your table for the Thanksgiving holiday, or as a hostess gift too!

I have used two new inductees into the language of flowers dictionary in this posy: white sage and wooly bush. White sage stands for purification of space and health. This meaning was easy to come up with because white sage has been considered a sacred plant for centuries and gives cleansing, protection, and purification. I added health because of the positive after-effects that occur when you cleanse your space with the smoke of this valuable herb. Wooly bush stands for tolerance and forgiveness because of its growth habits and endurance. Native to the western coast of Australia, it can tolerate salt and wind and can still thrive—hence "forgiveness."

Ingredients used are available in the summer and fall garden

3–5 stems Chrysanthemum: *cheerfulness, long life*

5–9 stems Mint: *warmth of feeling*

3–7 stems Rose: *love, beauty, friendship*

3–5 stems White Sage: *purification of space, health*

3–5 stems Alstromeria: *friendship*

1 stem Hydrangea: *haven, protection*

5–7 stems Cestrum: *transient beauty*

5–7 stems Wooly Bush: *forgiveness, tolerance*

5–7 stems Safflower: *welcome*

ALTERNATE INGREDIENTS AND SEASONAL VARIATIONS:

Dahlia (fall): *gratitude*

Pear (spring, summer, fall): *affection, health, hope, longevity*

Yellow Lily (summer): *happiness, gratitude, magnificent beauty*

Sweet Marjoram (spring, summer, fall): *joy, kindness*

Paperwhite Narcissus (winter, spring): *sweetness, you are sweet*

Phalaenopsis Orchid (year-round greenhouse): *evening joy*

DESIGN TIP:
The chrysanthemum in this posy is flat and open-faced, so it can be a bit of a challenge to have it work into the arrangement and still have the pavé affect. Slide these types of flowers into the posy from the top, after most of the other ingredients are in place, using the tops of stronger materials to hold the petals up.

Wooly Bush

Safflower

Cestrum

Hydrangea

Alstromeria

Chrysanthemum

Rose

Mint

White Sage

THE HOLIDAY WARMTH POSY

What a heartwarming posy to share with family and friends during the most wonderful time of the year! Rosemary, for remembrance, adds a nostalgic touch, triggering wonderful memories of holidays gone by, and the buds are a promise of good things to come, so this posy can carry well-wishes into the new year too. A Holiday Warmth Posy will make a beautiful centerpiece or side-table arrangement during holiday festivities, as well as a perfect host gift. And when your guests read the sentiment tag on this posy, they'll fall in love with it all over again.

⇒ Ingredients used are available in the fall and winter garden ⇐

1–3 stems Hydrangea: *haven*

7–9 stems Pineapple Sage: *hospitality*

5–7 stems Cedar: *strength*

3–5 stems Cotton: *well-being, blessings*

8–12 stems Spurge: *welcome*

7–9 stems Baby's Breath: *festivity*

6–8 stems Red Rose: *charm, joy*

3–5 stems Alstromeria: *friendship*

5–7 stems Rosemary: *remembrance*

6–9 stems Larkspur: *cheerfulness, fun*

3–5 stems Buds (any kind): *promise of good things to come*

ALTERNATE INGREDIENTS AND SEASONAL VARIATIONS:

Lemon Balm (summer): *fun*

Peony (spring, early summer): *welcome*

Olives (late summer): *peace and prosperity*

Hellebores (winter, spring): *a beautiful year ahead*

Mugwort (summer): *tranquility, happiness, peace*

Chinese Fringe Flower (summer): *merriment, joyful*

Holly Berries (winter): *Christmas joy, protection*

Cotton! This is a new entry into the modern dictionary. The meaning of well-being and blessings stems from the old idea that if you could harvest a good crop of cotton, you were blessed, hence the phrase "high-cotton." Cotton is a beautiful companion in a holiday posy; its appearance reminds us of snow, and coupled with baby's breath, it gives a feel of flurries on a cold winter's day.

Alstromeria

Red Rose

Baby's Breath

Hydrangea

Buds

Cotton

Larkspur

Rosemary

Spurge

Pineapple Sage

Cedar

A MOTHER'S LOVE

From the earliest days of childhood, we've gathered flowers for our mothers. Our tiny hands pulling, squeezing, and gathering—trying our best not to crinkle the blossoms—and we always presented our treasures with a smile, kiss, and hug.

If you haven't gathered flowers for your mother before, here is your chance. A posy for a mother (or grandmother) will melt her heart. And with a vast array of flowers to choose from with messages that carry profound sentiments of what she means to you, you just can't go wrong when creating this posy.

→ Ingredients used are available in the spring and summer garden ←

7–12 stems Sage: *greatest wisdom and respect*

3–6 stems Wisteria: *daughter's sweetness*

5–7 stems Snapdragon: *gracious lady, strength*

7–9 stems Scented Geranium: *gentility*

3–5 stems Honeysuckle: *generous and devoted affection*

5–7 stems Queen Anne's Lace: *haven, protection*

6–9 stems Cornflower: *refinement, devotion*

6–8 stems Rose: *love, beauty, friendship*

ALTERNATE INGREDIENTS AND SEASONAL VARIATIONS:

White Hollyhock (summer): *female ambition*

Jasmine (spring, summer, fall): *grace*

Water Lily (summer): *beauty, wisdom*

Pomegranate Flower (spring, early summer): *mature elegance*

Pussy-willow (spring, summer): *never-ceasing remembrance, motherhood*

Sequoia (year-round): *long life, vast wisdom*

The choice of flowers and their meanings are incredibly endearing in this posy. This is what floriography is about. You simply cannot try to articulate your feelings with words and come away with the same effect you'll have when you create a posy like this. Just look at all the delightful meanings this posy has! Any mother or grandmother would be enamored and overcome with emotion at receiving a gift like this.

Snap Dragon

Rose

Sage

Cornflower

Wisteria

Scented Geranium

Honeysuckle

Queen Anne's Lace

Healing Thoughts
Dill: soothing
Fern: sincerity
Peach: longevity
Abutilon: meditation
Dahlia: gratitude
Feverfew: good health
Solidaster: encouragement

HEALING THOUGHTS

How often do you want to send a get-well card to someone but feel like that's too generic? Instead, try making a Healing Thoughts Posy and leaving this beauty on their doorstep. When someone is under the weather, or fighting a more serious health battle, this posy sends them the message that yes, I can do this, and through love, support, and friends I can win. It is so important to support a friend, colleague, or anyone you love and care about with healing thoughts, and more important that you let them know about these thoughts. Using flowers to convey these messages, especially during trying times, can have a very powerful positive effect.

—⟩ Ingredients used are available in the summer garden ⟨—

8–12 stems Fern: *sincerity*

5–7 stems Solidaster: *encouragement*

3–5 stems Peach: *longevity*

5–7 stems Abutilon: *meditation*

3–5 stems Dahlia: *gratitude*

7–12 stems Feverfew: *good health*

ALTERNATE INGREDIENTS AND SEASONAL VARIATIONS:

Delphinium (summer): *well-being*

Calendula (spring, summer): *health*

Bachelor's Button (summer): *healing properties*

Garden Anemone (summer, fall): *belief, faith*

Elderberry (fall): *compassion, kindness*

Horehound (summer, fall): *virtue, fire*

Sometimes a simple, handwritten sentiment tag offers the perfect touch. For this posy it works well because the container is white, as is the tag background. This gives the overall presentation a little more formality, but with the added charm of a handwritten note.

Dill

Abutilon

Dahlia

Peach

Solidaster

Feverfew

THE FORTITUDE POSY

The Fortitude Posy stands in for such a wide array of emotions and can be used for many different occasions and milestones. Highly textural, it's a very complex and interesting posy to look at. The variations of shapes and sizes of the materials create a captivating floral arrangement. The sentiments in this posy are moving and very uplifting—*strength, protection, sincerity, love,* and more. This is the posy I sent to my dad after he suffered a stroke. When someone you love and care about is experiencing trials and tribulations, the Fortitude Posy will lift their spirits and show you love and care like nothing else. In my case, this posy conveyed its particular sentiments, as well as my personal concern for my dad, in a way that I could have never articulated in words.

Ingredients used are available in the summer and fall garden

5–8 stems Cestrum: *transient beauty*

1 stem Protea: *loyalty*

3 stems Hypericum: *protection*

5 stems Bamboo: *strength*

7–9 stems Fern: *sincerity*

3–5 stems Grevillea: *steadfastness*

3 stems Aeonium (Hens and Chicks): *vivacity*

5–7 stems Rose: *love, beauty*

7–9 stems Mint: *warmth of feeling*

ALTERNATE INGREDIENTS AND SEASONAL VARIATIONS:

Lady's Mantle (summer): *comforting love*

Angelica (summer): *inspiration*

Queen Anne's Lace (summer): *haven, sanctuary, warmth*

Japanese Quince (spring): *prosperity, symbolic of luck, good fortune, love*

Cedar (year-round): *strength, prosperity, drives away negative energies*

Bronze Chrysanthemum (fall): *joy, truth, friendship*

Grevillea

Aeonium

Rose

Cestrum

Mint

Bamboo

Hypericum

Protea

Fern

IN SYMPATHY POSY

Flowers used in sympathy floriography are astoundingly powerful and always well received. A grieving period is one of the most meaningful times to send your thoughts and love to someone who is experiencing a loss, because no spoken word can articulate as beautifully as flowers with their sentiments.

➤ Ingredients used are available in the spring and summer garden ⭠

5–7 stems White Roses: *love, respect*

7–12 stems Heath Myrtle: *sustenance, adversity*

5–7 stems Narcissus ("Early Cheer" variety shown here): *hope*

6–8 stems Rosemary: *remembrance*

5–7 stems Pansy: *you occupy my thoughts*

7–12 stems Lamb's Ears: *softness, support*

5–8 stems Sweet Pea: *delicate pleasures, departure*

ALTERNATE INGREDIENTS AND SEASONAL VARIATIONS:

Forget-Me-Not (spring): *remembrance*

Balm (summer): *sympathy*

White Periwinkle (summer): *pleasure of memory*

Yarrow (summer): *cure for heartache*

Thrift (summer): *sympathy*

Lily of the Valley (spring): *return of happiness*

Weeping Willow (year-round): *mourning*

Yew (year-round): *sorrow*

DESIGN TIP:

Pansies are so beautiful in posies, but their stems can be very short. Try and select the blooms with the longest stems, and then place them into the posy last, right before you tie off your bouquet. Because the blooms are so delicate, as well as the stems, you don't want them placed into the posy while you're still forming and shaping it. The blooms look nice tucked into the top, with the petals resting on other flowers for support. People want to see the beautiful pansy face too!

In Sympathy

White Rose; *love, respect*

Pansy; *thoughts*

Sweet Pea; *delicate pleasures, departure*

Narcissus; *hope*

Rosemary; *remembrance*

Lamb's Ears; *support*

Heath Myrtle; *sustenance, adversity*

Lamb's Ears

Sweet Pea

White Rose

Heath Myrtle

Pansy

Rosemary

Narcissus

THE STAY STRONG POSY

Sometimes, life throws us distressing situations that we must deal with. It's hard, and there are times we feel like—how am I going to get through this?

The Stay Strong Posy is another fine example of how flowers and their eloquent and heartfelt messages can say what we need to say better than any spoken word.

Ingredients used are available in the spring and summer garden

5–7 stems Hawthorne: *hope*

7–9 stems Cedar: *strength*

4–6 stems Silver Tree Leucodendron: *steadfastness*

6–7 stems Yellow Rose: *caring, friendship*

4–6 stems Abutilon: *meditation*

7–12 stems Dill (here I have used leaves): *soothing*

6–9 stems Bouvardia: *enthusiasm*

ALTERNATE INGREDIENTS AND SEASONAL VARIATIONS:

Yarrow (summer, fall): *cure for heartache*

Wandering Jew Plant (year-round houseplant): *felicity, happiness*

Loquat (summer, fall): *personal warmth and comfort*

Spruce Pine (year-round): *hope in adversity*

Silver King Artemisia (spring, summer, fall): *happiness, power, dignity*

Heath Myrtle (spring, summer): *sustenance, adversity*

I have seen firsthand the reactions of family and friends that have looked at a beautiful posy and then absorbed its sentiment, and they are always priceless. No one can ever estimate how strong and powerful of an effect the language of flowers will have on another person, but you can also never doubt there will be a strong and positive outcome, and that is because of the thoughts you are conveying and effort you have put into your gift of a posy.

Yellow Rose

Bouvardia

Dill

Cedar

Hawthorne

Silvertree

Abutilon

HAPPY DAYS

Along with the Stay Strong Posy, here a two more examples of posies that can give cheer and uplifting messages for someone who needs a pick-me-up. Numerous flowers convey inspiring messages, so a cheer up posy is always a quick and easy posy to create.

Vibrant colors say *happy*, so using a bright color palette when making a posy with an intention to cheer someone up is a good idea. Luckily, there are fantastic options with appropriate cheerful meanings in bright and happy colors.

Ingredients used are available in the spring and summer garden

5–7 stems Ceanothus: *vibrant personality*
5 stems Freesia: *thoughtfulness*
3–5 stems Forsythia: *good nature*
4–6 stems Bouvardia: *enthusiasm*

4–6 stem Cinaria: *ever bright, always delighted*
5–7 stems Hawthorne: *hope*

THE CHEER UP POSY

The Cheer Up Posy includes lamb's ears, which convey the message of softness and support. Sometimes a more subtle message is appropriate when the occasion calls for a quiet and meaningful gesture. Either way, bright and happy, or soft and supportive, Cheer Up Posies hit the mark when it comes to helping someone get out of a down-low state, and into happier thoughts.

With just four ingredients, you can make a beautiful and heartfelt token of caring. Posies do not have to be a big and complicated chore! Just a few ingredients with good meanings, arranged nicely and presented with a little smile can make all the difference!

Ingredients used are available in the winter and spring garden

3 stems Hellebores: *a beautiful year ahead*   4–5 stems Lamb's Ears: *softness, support*
2–3 stems Pieris: *happy thoughts*
1–2 stems Forsythia: *good nature*

Pieris   *Hellebores*

Forsythia   *Lamb's Ears*

Making Posies

The idea for me to begin my business as a florist started in the garden. I believe the inspiration that nature can provide is a fantastic jump start to the creation of a posy (either for yourself or for someone else). If possible, start in a place of nature. That can be your porch, patio, backyard, a public garden, or even a garden book or magazine if you can't get physically into that place. Posies are generally "garden-inspired" bouquets that carry beautiful poetical sentiments, so putting yourself in that environment will trigger your inspirations.

Once you become inspired and excited by beautiful flowers in the garden, or at another outlet, but before you begin to cut (or buy) your ingredients, try and piece together the posy and its sentiments in your mind. If there is a specific occasion that you want to make a posy for, then your goal will be to cut and collect ingredients according to that sentiment or occasion. When I first began making posies, I would go into the garden and start cutting things that were in heavy bloom and looked beautiful to me. And this is ok to do, if that flower has a sentiment that you can use for your occasion or overall message. You can make a posy out of whatever is pretty at the time, but just be aware that each individual flower's sentiment might not work with the overall sentiment or occasion, making it difficult to create a true posy that conveys a message using the language of flowers.

It helps if you can take a walk through the garden, yard, or patio, and check out what you have on hand and ready to cut. Sometimes this may be a skewed choice of greens, herbs, or inconspicuous flowers, which would require you to outsource a focal and complementary flower or your greenery. Alternately, if you've been to the florist, farmer's market, or supermarket and purchased a beautiful grower's bunch of roses, tulips, or other primary focal flowers, this will give you a jump start, and all you'll need to do then is gather your greens, herbs, and perhaps a complementary flower or other element.

Any sentiment and any occasion can be marked by creating a posy. I give posies to people for the smallest occasions up to the grandest and most important milestones of life. A posy is always well-received because of its value as a cordial and highly personalized gift. Sometimes, I love to make a posy for myself! It's a form a self-care and works magic on my mental state, and it's good for me physically, too. When I make myself a posy I'm usually meditating about a decision or need a little pick-me-up—something to remind myself that with all of life's ups and downs, it is still a beautiful world.

START WITH THE SENTIMENT

The idea of a posy is to create a message using the language of flowers. There are different ways you can start the process of making a posy. Of course, you can utilize the recipes I've created in the previous section, but you can also start the creation of your posy in a more self-guided way.

You can decide what flowers and plants are available to you from various sources—either in the garden, at the farmer's market, or at the local florist,

and use the *New Language of Flowers Dictionary* (page 151) as your guide to create a cohesive sentiment or message. The dictionary is quite extensive and the more you read it and learn, the more inspired you will become while discovering all the flowers, plants, and trees that have meanings attached to them. Personally, I love to use the dictionary when thinking about the ingredients I want to use in a posy. You will find many flowers and plants to use, and sometimes feel there are too many ingredients to choose from! This is a nice problem to have, because this is when you can get very selective according to color and texture, allowing you to achieve the desired aesthetic of your posy. As you will see in the dictionary, there can be several meanings to one flower, plant, or herb. When using a plant that has several meanings attached to it, choose one or two meanings that fit the sentiment of your posy. For instance, when you are creating a sympathy posy and you would like to use thyme, which has several meanings attached to it—activity, bravery, and courage—it would be fitting to use the meaning of *courage*.

To narrow your options, you can start with the *Quick-Start Occasions Directory* (page 237), which lists various occasions with flowers that carry meanings appropriate to each occasion. Using this directory is extremely helpful when you don't have the time to review the dictionary for your ingredients. All you do is look for the occasion you want to make a posy for and you will find a reference point for several flowers, including focal and complementary flowers, as well as herbs and greens that would be appropriate to use for your chosen occasion.

Alternately, start with the *Quick-Start Sentiments Directory* (page 239), which lists various sentiments and emotions, and use several options from there to create your posy. This directory is a perfect tool to use when you are trying to express specific thoughts or emotions. I recently had a friend whose husband was dying of cancer. It was a long and difficult struggle for them both. I felt her pain, and I wanted to make a posy for her. All I could do was look through the sentiments directory to mark all the feelings and thoughts I wanted to send her during this very challenging and sad time. Her posy ended up being one of strength, love, and endurance. Essentially, it said to her *just hang in there, and I love you*. Times like these are the perfect times to use the *Quick-Start Sentiments Directory*.

The fragrance of the rose lingers on the hand that cast it
—*William Shakespeare*

HOW TO MAKE A POSY

Choose a workspace that has well-lit, but not too direct light, along with a good amount of clear space. You can protect any wood table by using a vinyl tablecloth as there will be plant debris and water on it.

Equipment

To make a posy, you will need:

- Floral shears: both snippers and bunch cutters

- Scissors

- Watering can

- Garden twine

- Disposable gloves

- 2 or 3 small buckets filled with clean, room temperature water

- Selected posy container filled with clean water and prepared with commercial flower food

Flower and Plant Material

A posy is a bunch of flowers artfully arranged, tied off, and placed into a vase, with a finished size of approximately 6 to 8 inches in circumference. You will be the one to decide which flowers, herbs, and plants you use in your posy, based upon their meaning, color, and texture. The varying number of ingredients that I recommend using would depend upon the visual appearance they give off when combined.

You will need 5 to 9 different plant ingredients, and anywhere from 3 to 9 stems of each of those.

- **Focal flowers:** 1 or 2 varieties and 3 to 7 stems of each (depending on size of bloom)

- **Complementary flowers:** 2–4 varieties and 3 to 9 stems of each

- **Herbs:** 1 or 2 varieties and 3 to 9 stems of each

- **Greens:** 1 or 2 varieties and 3 to 9 stems of each

The finished posy should impart an aesthetically balanced floral arrangement—it should be easy on the eye, and pleasant to look at. Posies are small in nature, so it is important to organize your arrangement appropriately. Using these four design tips when selecting your ingredients will help you to achieve the hallmark of good floral design, hence a beautiful posy.

1. **Balanced color:** It is best to stick to a monochromatic or analogous color scheme. Monochromatic is defined as using various tints and shades of a single color. Analogous is defined as using 2 to 4 hues that are neighboring on the color wheel.

2. **Variety of texture:** A variety of texture in a posy avoids monotony and creates interest.

3. **Proportionate Ingredients:** A posy should have several stems of a focal flower, a few more of a complementary flower, a few sprigs of herbs and greenery. Too many of one type of these ingredients will result in an unbalanced or chaotic feel to your posy.

4. **Pavé Shaped:** Pavé is a method of "paving" with flowers. When designing in pavé style, there should not be any protruding blooms or other elements coming out from the top of the posy. The posy should be rounded—dome shaped and smooth. The pavé shape is an important element in setting your posy apart from other flower arrangements.

It also pays homage to the historical tradition of a posy being a small, circular gathering of flowers, plants, and herbs, while giving it a modern and up-to-date style. Creating the pavé style takes some practice, but the result is captivating and highly impactful due to the smaller size of a posy, because you're packing in a lot of texture and eye-candy.

FLOWER TYPES AND DESCRIPTIONS

Focal Flowers

The focal flowers for posies fall into the *mass* and *form* flower categories for traditional flower arrangements. Form, mass, and focal flowers are all referred to as **focal** flowers in this book. These flowers are used to create the shape and outline in a posy.

In floral design terms, mass flowers are usually rounded in shape, and include, but are not limited to, roses, carnations, and chrysanthemums. Form flowers are flowers with a special feature that can draw attention and are usually more expensive than mass flowers. Other examples of focal flowers are calla lilies, orchids, dahlias, and gardenias.

Complementary Flowers

Complementary flowers are usually referred to as "fillers" in floral design terms and can be used to cover gaps and fill spaces in an arrangement. I have never liked the term "filler" because they are still flowers, and are ripe with meaning. So, instead, I call these complementary flowers, because they complement the focal flower visually and with their sentiments. Some examples of complementary flowers are baby's breath, solidaster, and alstromeria.

Line Flowers

Line flowers are tall, slender stemmed flowers used to create structure in flower arrangements and can serve as complementary flowers in posies. They have indeterminate blooms going consecutively upward on the stem. When using line flowers in posies, you will need to "top-off" the stems, so the prominent lower flowers can be seen in the posy, instead of the small, unopened blossoms that appear atop the line flowers (see instructions on page 135). Some examples of line flowers are larkspur, Bells of Ireland, and snapdragons.

*Focal flower:
Camellia is also
considered a form
flower*

*Focal flower:
Pincushion Protea is
also considered a form
flower*

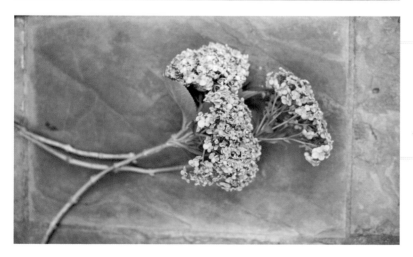

*Focal flower:
Hydrangea is also
considered a mass
flower*

Complementary flower:
Calcynia

Complementary flower:
Chocolate Cosmo

Complementary flower:
Sweet Pea

Line flower: Stock

Line flower: Delphinium

Line flower: Tuberose

Herbs and Greens

In some styles of floral design, "greens" are used primarily as for coverage to hide the not-so-attractive containers (plastic trays) and floral foam. This is unfortunate because foliage is so beautiful and can be incorporated so nicely into the arrangement. When making a posy, you'll use herbs and greenery—foliage—as an integral part of the flower arrangement. Foliage carries so many sentiments and messages that often cannot be represented by any flower. When creating your posy, often the foliage is the material you'll use as a "collar," a decoration around the edges of the posy to frame it nicely.

Some other examples of foliage (or "collar materials") are scented geranium, fern, heuchera leaves, oregano, and rosemary. Since herbs and greenery can be the workhorse of the posy, carrying messages just as important as the flowers, it's a good idea to include at least a couple of different types of them in your posy.

Bamboo

Rue (herb)

Flower Types

Inflorescence is the term used to describe a flower type, and simply refers to how the flowers are arranged on the stem. When making a posy, it is a good practice to balance out the inflorescence types by using 3 to 4 types in your posy.

- **Solitary**: One bloom per stem, such as roses and tulips

- **Spray**: Multiple flowers per stem, such as spray roses and lisianthus

- **Inflorescence**: This is where it gets a bit confusing. Inflorescence is the general term for how flowers are arranged on the stem, but it also describes flowers where there is a complete flower head on the stem, such as hydrangea and Queen Anne's lace.

- **Spike**: Long stems with smaller flowers on them, such as foxglove, delphinium, and snapdragons

GATHERING AND CONDITIONING FLOWERS

The care and conditioning of your flowers will determine the life of your flowers. It is so important to treat your cut flowers right from the beginning. Before you can use your plant material and flowers, either brought in from the garden or another source, they must be prepped. The purpose of the preparation of your flowers is to prevent air bubbles in the stems, rotting material on the stem or in the vase water, and to enable the plant to hydrate the blossom, instead of leaf material. Sometimes the best flowers to use for a posy are landscaping flowers, because of their sentiment, but they don't always make the best cut flowers. To use landscaping or wild flowers when making a posy, you'll have to prep them very diligently so that they give a decent vase life. In floristry, we knowingly use flowers that have extraordinarily short vase life, because of their beauty and/or their scent. I think the ephemeral beauty adds to their exquisiteness. It means you'll need to take the time to really look at them, smell them, marvel at them, and enjoy them during their short stay in the vase.

Harvesting Garden Flowers

First, *a note of caution.* All plants and flowers have liquid compounds in their stems and leaves. Most of these compounds are harmless when it comes into contact with the skin, however, some are highly volatile and may cause a reaction on your skin. Some of these compounds are clear and seemingly harmless (sumac), and some are milky and obviously toxic. For this reason, I recommend to always use disposable gloves when cutting and arranging your flowers and plant material. You may not always have to use gloves, but until you know which plant materials adversely affect you, it's a good idea to protect your skin. And under any circumstances, never touch your face, especially your eyes, after handling flower and plant material without a thorough hand wash. After a long time in floristry, I've compiled a list of known culprits that have caused mild to moderate dermatitis:

- Amaranth
- Alstromeria (rarely, but can cause mild dermatitis)
- Dogbane, includes all "bane" family members (wolfbane, periwinkle, oleander, blue star, aclepias, swallowwort, silkvine)
- Euphorbia, (includes spurge) all varieties
- Milkweed
- Sumac, including smoke bush and strawberry sumac
- Tweedia
- Platycodon (balloon flower)
- Poppy

When and How to Cut Your Garden Flowers and Greens

Always cut your flowers in the morning or evening. This is the time when the moisture content is at its highest in the bloom, and the time when the sun is not at its hottest stage.

Use clean and very sharp cutting shears and cut at a sharp angle so that more surface area is available to uptake water.

When selecting a stem to cut from a plant, try for the stems that are becoming woody, rather than for fresh grown green stems. When a stem is getting woody, you'll see tiny brown specks appearing up the stem. Tender shoots of mint for example, with their fresh and new green growth, will wilt quickly and may not recover from the cut. This can get tricky though, because if the stem is going woody, that means the bloom has been present longer too, so you must take care not to cut blooms that are too open or looking aged. Sometimes hydrangea will still wilt even though you've done everything right. If that's the case, submerge the entire head of florets under room-temperature water and let the cells in the florets fill up with water for 15 minutes.

Prepping and Conditioning Your Flowers

It's best to remove all leaf material as you go, directly after the cut. If you cannot do that, then as soon as possible remove all lower leaves and side-shoots from the stems. This is done for two reasons: when the water travels up the stem, we want it to hydrate the bloom. If you have all the leaf material still attached to the stem, some of the hydration will go to the leaves rather than the bloom. Also, you do not want leaf material under the water in the bucket, as it promotes bacterial growth.

If you're using line flowers, this is the time to prepare them by topping them off. To top off line flowers, simply snip off the top down to the first set of prominent blooms.

This delphinium is ready to use; it has been topped-off, and all lower blossoms and foliage have been removed.

If you are using flowers that require wiring, such as gardenias or camellia, now is the time to wire these blooms into place with florist's wire and tape.

After you've prepped all your flowers and greens, it's time for conditioning. Ideally you should condition your flowers before using them, which entails setting them in deep water for 2 to 4 hours in a cool, dark place. During this time, they are basically taking a relaxing bath and trying to hydrate themselves. The conditioning period can happen after the posy is made by setting your completed posy in a cool, dark place prior to sending off to its destination. This is ok as long as you are not using very tender greens and flowers. The very tender greens and delicate flowers tend to really need a conditioning period. (However, if you are really in a rush, you can skip the conditioning period—I have used flowers to make my posies directly after cutting them when time is of the essence.)

Tulips, daffodils, and hyacinths need a little special conditioning. The very light green part of the stem at the very bottom needs to be cut off, as it does not take up water. Flowers with milky sap in their stems, such as daffodils, tweedia, and euphorbia, need to be conditioned separately as their sap leaks into the water, which causes other flowers to deteriorate. Set these milky-sapped flowers in a separate bucket with deep water to let them bleed out before combining into the other buckets of flowers.

Note that it is very difficult to use tulips in posies with other flowers. Tulips continue to grow after you cut them, and they are phototropic, meaning they bend toward the light. They will look nice in your posy for a short time, but within hours they will begin to shoot upward above all the rest of your materials, and then they will begin to turn toward where there is light. It's best to use tulips as a mono-botanical posy.

Poppies and euphorbia can be seared at the bottom with a match or lighter to prevent their sap from coagulating and blocking water uptake.

Woody-stemmed flowers such as lilac need an extremely slanted cut to ensure water uptake, and also a split-cut up the center of the stem. You can achieve this by making your cut at a strongly slanting angle, and then holding the stem straight up-and-down and making a cut from the bottom directly upward the center of the stem. Some instructions will recommend pounding woody stems with a hammer, but I do not endorse this method as it will clog the stem with dead cells and prevent water uptake.

The leaves of scented geraniums have a large, soft surface area that can dry out very quickly and cause wilting. Directly after cutting, remove all the unwanted lower branching leaves, and lay the entire stem and leaves submerged in a dish of tepid water. Try to leave it submerged for at least 10 to 20 minutes, and longer if possible. This technique will allow the tissues in the leaves to absorb the water and prevent wilting. Note that this technique will not work with gray or downy-leafed foliage, as the hairy surface prevents moisture uptake.

CONTAINERS

The perfect posy container would be approximately 6 to 8 inches tall and 5 inches deep, with a 3.5-inch opening.

All the containers pictured above work well for setting a posy inside. I adore using footed containers and goblets for the simple reason that they elevate the posy and put it into good view. It's also so easy to attach your sentiment card to a goblet because it will hang down nicely.

PUTTING IT ALL TOGETHER

I selected these ingredients because most of them are readily available from the spring and summer garden. To me, the meanings of these flowers felt perfect for the person I was giving the posy to, and I especially love the color combinations.

6 stems Coral Sweetheart roses *(focal flower)*

6 stems heath myrtle *(complementary flower)*

5 stems fir *(foliage)*

5 stems delphinium *(complementary flower)*

6 stems red geranium *(complementary flower)*

5 stems geranium leaves *(for collar)*

DESIGN TIPS

A posy is a tied-off bunch of flowers, set in a vase, with a finished size of 6 to 9 inches in diameter. These tips will help you achieve the desired look of your posy.

- It helps to use odd numbers in focal flowers, but this does not always apply if you're using a larger focal flower. Do what you think looks best as far as how many focal flowers to use. The result should be aesthetically appealing and stay in line with the four golden rules:

  ⟫ 1. A good balance of texture

  ⟫ 2. Harmonious colors: think of the color wheel. I like to use monochromatic or analogous colors together, or sometimes complementary

  ⟫ 3. Not too many herbs versus focal and complementary flowers, or otherwise your posy will have a weedy or chaotic look and feel to it

  ⟫ 4. A finished pavé-style posy

- When using disk-shaped flowers with wide, flat heads such as Queen Anne's lace, scabiosa, and some heliotropes, you'll need to work them in between other flowers that have already been placed. This helps to hold up and support the discoid shape.

- Cut some of the stem length down on your materials while you're forming your posy. You want approximately 12 inches of stem left on, so that you can fresh-cut the stems after your posy is finished.

- Try to always have the flowers prepped completely. It can be difficult to remove outshoots and excess blooms from the bottom part of line flowers while you are forming the posy in your hands.

STEP 1

Arrange all your prepared ingredients out in front of you, organized by material type, and have your tools ready.

STEP 2

Begin to form your posy by creating a central pivot. Use one of your focal flowers, 1 to 3 of your complementary flowers depending on their size, and 2 to 3 herb sprigs if you have them in your recipe. The central pivot will end up being the middle point in your finished posy.

STEP 3

Work from the central pivot outward with a grouping of each of your materials except for the collar material (that goes around the outer perimeter of your finished posy). Holding your starting pivot grouping in one hand, start to build outward with your other hand by adding another focal, then a sprig or two of an herb around that, then place a complementary flower or two on the outer edges of that, then another focal with some herbs and complementary flowers around that. The goal is to disperse the different material types evenly throughout the posy.

To maintain the pavé shape, keep an eye on the top level of each of the ingredients you add. Each time you add an ingredient, it should be placed a little lower than the inward placements. Be mindful of the directions of the blooms—sometimes they are facing more in one direction than the other. You should turn them all to where they will face the outside of the posy.

STEP 4

Greenery or an herb that has a frilly edge is great "collar" material. Posies look best when you form a collar along the outer edges because it helps to frame your posy and highlight the flowers and materials used. Your collar material is part of the posy and has a meaning, but is also helpful in covering and disguising the vase line. You never want to see the vase/container top line in floral design. The flower arrangement and top line of the container should blend together.

STEP 5

Using a grower's tie method, bind the stems in place: Use regular garden twine, and place one end under a finger that is up high along the stems, leaving approximately 3 inches extra "tail." Wrap the twine snuggly as high up on the posy as you can—go around twice and finish where the two end pieces can be knotted together.

Sometimes, during the tying off process, some stems can shift out of place. Look at the posy from all angles and ensure it's not lopsided or crooked. If you are pleased with the shape, then finish by snipping off the extra twine.

Alternately, you can bind the stems together with florist's tape. This may be helpful when you have a very small opening in your container. Binding with tape will squeeze the stems together and hold them in place so that you can fit the stems into a smaller container. Start by placing the binding tape horizontally along the very highest point along the stems—directly under the collar material. Gently squeeze together the stems while you wrap the binding tape around 3 to 5 times.

Once you have the posy securely tied off, then you need to cut down the stems. Using your bunch cutters, cut your stems below the twine or tape, leaving enough for the stems to be near the bottom of your container but not touching.

Set your posy into your selected container to see how it fits. You want your posy to sit on the edges of the container, not standing on the stems. Fluff the collar around the edges so you disguise the top line of the container.

STEP 6

Once your posy is made and tied off, it's time to package it up for a beautiful presentation. Be sure to dress it up! Packaging and presentation are just as important as the posy itself. Your posy is not complete without beautiful packing and presentation—this is what will set your posy apart from a standard flower arrangement. The container, ribbon, and sentiment tag you choose will give your posy a finished look and create the appearance of a well-packaged gift.

THE SENTIMENT TAG

The sentiment tag is what makes a posy *a posy*. If you don't have a sentiment tag on your posy, it will only be a beautiful flower arrangement. No one will realize that you have created a message especially for them with your carefully chosen flowers, plants, and herbs. So, you must tell them!

The sentiment tags are attached to the posy by stringing them up through a hole in the tag, to hang on the tail of your ribbon. I like to write the names of all the flowers I have used, followed by their definitions on the front side of the sentiment tag, and then on the back side I offer a brief explanation of what a posy is. For example:

> *A posy is a petite arrangement of flowers, plants, and herbs that convey a message in the language of flowers. This posy was made especially for you! What is your posy saying to you?*

Your sentiment tag should be about 2.5 inches wide and 3.5 inches long, but it can vary a little. Use the size that makes sense and looks right for the posy and its container. It looks best when the sentiment tag hangs free, without touching the surface the posy is sitting on, so consider that when you're deciding the size of your tag.

Sentiment tags are your opportunity to get crafty, and there are several ways to make them. You can start simple with a piece of card stock cut to the right size. You can also cut out the front side of greeting cards—they're so pretty! Use the back side to write your sentiment message. Feel free to embellish it more with trims and baubles or leave it the way it is.

Sentiment tags can be simple, easy, and pretty. You don't have to go through a lot of trouble if you're not into crafting and embellishing. Here is an example of a simple but pretty tag that was printed on a home-office printer using the downloadable sentiment tags from my website, teresasabankaya.com.

A small adornment on the edge adds an elegant and slightly whimsical touch to your sentiment tags. Don't get too serious—let your creative juices flow!

I enjoy the creative process of embellishing my sentiment tags. Using vintage trims, sequins, and baubles adds so much to the tags, which are already a very important part of a posy. I always like to think of the sentiment tags as keepsakes that will be cherished by the recipient long after the posy fades.

RIBBONS

I love ribbons! If you're a ribbon and textile lover, then you'll enjoy packaging your posy with beautiful ribbon work. Some ribbons work better than others for posies, and some I would absolutely stay away from. It's difficult to use wired ribbon: it will not hang naturally and gives a stiff appearance in contrast to a delicate posy. It's also difficult to string the sentiment tag up the ribbon tail of a wired ribbon.

And a wide ribbon is difficult to use because it will stretch the punch hole of your sentiment tag and tear it.

I like to use a double-faced satin because its weight is perfect for holding a bow, but soft enough to give an elegant flow on the bow and tails. Most of the time, I use a satin ribbon with a width of ⅜ inch.

To make a bow for your posy, you'll need approximately 36 inches length of ribbon. Start by making a 2-inch diameter loop, leaving a tail of approximately 6 inches. Then, create another 2-inch loop opposite the first, using the longer side of the ribbon. Repeat on each side three times, then secure with either a pipe cleaner, or florist's wire.

Now, you'll need to attach the bow to the posy by tucking the ends of the wire into the stems of the posy, behind the binding twine.

If your sentiment tag does not already have a punched hole to hang it from, punch a hole at the top. Be sure to leave a little extra space from the edge in case of a small tear or some stretching when the ribbon is pulled through the hole.

If you are using a footed container such as a goblet, you can tie your ribbon directly to the stem of the container.

The New Language of Flowers Dictionary

"Oh, Tiger-Lily," said Alice, addressing herself to one that was gracefully waving in the wind, "I wish you could talk!"

"We can talk," said the Tiger-Lily, "When there's anybody worth talking to."

—*Through the Looking-Glass, and What Alice Found There*, Lewis Carroll, 1871

Giving flowers their meanings has not fallen on the shoulders of one person. There were very early writers who began penning definitions in the first language of flower dictionaries, and then many writers afterward who created many more dictionaries to build on the founding ones. Through time, we have been left with copious amounts of dictionaries, gift books, and many other publications referencing the language of flowers. And so, there is no such thing as the one true language of flowers.

The entries in my *New Language of Flowers Dictionary* are compiled from early and late floral dictionaries, gift books, books on the symbolic meaning of flowers, and books on the history of the language of flowers, originating from French and British sources, as well as sources from Australia, New Zealand, China, and Japan. The *New Language of Flowers Dictionary* is an anthology built from all these references, as well as from internet searches that turned up everything from university research papers to blog posts and everything in between. Rather than creating a technical horticultural reference for plant identification, I developed this dictionary to serve as an artistic aide in using the language of flowers to create sentiments and be your one-stop shop for flower meanings, both historical and modern.

I am certainly not the first person to write a floral dictionary and will not be the last either. In fact, a floral dictionary with the language of flowers can never be completed! Every year, we add more newly hybridized flowers, plants, and trees to our horticulture plant list. According to a report released by Kew Gardens, 2,034 plants were discovered in 2015 alone, and there are now an estimated 390,900 plants known to science.

It was out of necessity that I created this modern dictionary. Through the years, I have found that while creating a posy, either to sell at my flower shop or for my own personal gift-giving, I will fall in love with a flower I want to use because of its beauty or because it lent itself nicely to a posy because of its bloom size, its unique coloring, or another aesthetic characteristic. But time and time again I could not find the flower's definition in any of my resources. When this was the case, and it was a flower or plant that I really wanted to incorporate into a posy, and was readily available to me, I created a meaning for it. I created a meaning just the way all the others before me did. I studied the look and aesthetic of the flower, noting its physical characteristics, as well as how it grows in its natural state in the garden or in the wild. I asked myself: are there any unique qualities about how this flower or plant grows? If so, I tried to apply the attribute to its new meaning. Or maybe the flower I wanted to use had a unique fragrance, or a strange leaf shape from which

I gathered a meaning. Again, these are specific attributes that I took into consideration. And more important, I always considered the genus, which told me which flowers the particular one I was interested in might be related to. The flowers I was drawn to in these cases were usually new hybrid flowers, and therefore they have parental lineage that I can follow back. What family do they belong to, I wondered, and what are some of their relatives that we know, and already have meanings for in the language of flowers? These are all the things I considered, researched, and studied before I made a new entry in the dictionary. Therefore, I refer to this dictionary as the *New Language of Flowers Dictionary*. I have simply expanded a reference guide for flowers, just as has been done many times before me, and this modern version holds meanings of some newer hybridized flowers and plants that we readily find in garden centers, grocery stores, flower farms, and flower shops—flowers that are ordinary to our everyday eye, but ones that may have never been defined in this particular way before now.

FASCINATING FLORIOGRAPHY

Through my years of practicing floriography, as well as researching for this book, I have discovered some very interesting and fun facts about the language of flowers, botany, and human nature. Our imaginations can be quite vivid and colorful, and the relationships we have with botany are captivating. I find it interesting how we've used human emotions, and sometimes quirky characteristics of our personalities, and applied them to equally quirky plants and flowers. For instance, the bladdernut tree has some peculiar-looking seed pods that resemble a human bladder—hence the name "bladdernut." Beyond this, the meaning in the ages-old language of flowers is *amusement* and *frivolity*, and the seed pods do look amusing, and frankly a little frivolous!

Asclepia, or butterfly weed—aka milkweed—means *let me go*. It's clear why it has been given this definition, as milkweed is very sticky, and it's not uncommon to see small insects stuck to its sappy, sticky stamens. The arborvitae is often used for hedging as it virtually never changes its stature and has a very slow growth rate. It is also evergreen, so its definitions of *unchanging friendship* and *tree of life* are very appropriate.

Some plants and flowers play very important roles in nature. One example is the lucerne, or alfalfa, which when looked up in Kate Greenaway's *Language of Flowers* means *life*. Of course it means life! Cattle and sheep have grazed and thrived on lucerne for centuries, and Greenaway's defnition seems so simple and direct. The plant is life-giving and there is really no stronger definition for it than *life*.

I have also found a few plants that I would use with great discretion due to their natural composition. Ambrosia is one such plant—it is ragweed! How awful to give a posy to someone that has ragweed in it! But its definition is quite lovely—*love returned*. Hmm. On the contrary, I would say!

So, the use of floriography extends beyond just the language of flowers, and single flower definitions. Each individual flower may have different meanings according to how they are encountered in nature and then placed in a posy, or how they are presented by the posy's maker, and then what action the recipient takes once the posy is received. According to Charles W. Seelye's 1878 book *The Language of Flowers and Floral Conversation*, there are some rules that must be followed when using floriography:

> **Rule 1:** If a flower is presented reversed [upside down], its original definition is understood to be contradicted, and the opposite meaning be implied.
>
> **Rule 2:** *Yes* is naturally expressed by touching the flower received with the lips.
>
> **Rule 3:** *No* is expressed by pinching off a petal or some small part and casting it away.
>
> **Rule 4:** The meaning of a flower may be used as a noun, as a verb, or as an adverb, as may be convenient. For example, the flowering almond expresses *hope*, but in connection with some other flower it may be *hopefully* or *to hope* in any tense.

And in addition to single flower variables, there are even different meanings associated with a bouquet of flowers, and how it is given and received from hand to hand. A bouquet given/accepted with the right hand means accepted, agreement, affirmation, and a bouquet given/accepted with the left hand means refusal, disagreement, a negative response.

Finally, a bouquet of withered flowers stands for *rejected love*.

So, throughout history, we have come up with some very clever and sometimes humorous definitions for flowers, plants, and even groups of them and how they are arranged. We've devised ways to define a flower's role as a symbol of certain beliefs, and even superstitions—as well as thoughts and emotions. Some devised meanings are very simple, and some are more complex and can take the lead from botanical characteristics or growth habits.

For example, the term *bane* comes from the Old English *bana*, meaning "thing causing death, poison." In botany, bane is an old element present in the common names of plants known to be toxic or poisonous. In the Middle Ages, several poisonous plants of the genus Aconitum were thought to have prophylactic qualities, repelling and protecting against that which they were banes to. So, dogbane would protect you from dogs, wolfbane from wolves, etc.

According to *Oxford English Dictionary*'s Ask Oxford site, a word with the suffix *-wort* is often very old, and you'll notice that this suffix is present in many plant names, such as mugwort. The Old English suffix, *wyrt*, from Proto-Indo-European origins connects it to *root*. It was often used in the names of herbs and plants that had medicinal uses, especially in the root, with the first part of the word denoting the complaint against which it might be especially efficacious.

HOW TO USE THE DICTIONARY

Because this new dictionary is a compilation, a single plant, tree, or flower can have many meanings and some of the meanings can contradict another. Do not feel that you cannot use a flower because it may have some definitions within the larger definition that aren't appropriate for your posy. You can choose to only use one definition that portrays your message, or several if you feel it's appropriate. And feel free to leave off any definitions that may contradict your overall sentiment.

You can use either the leaf or the flower of a particular plant to convey a message. All parts of the plant can be used in posies in representation of your sentiment, unless a particular part is noted as otherwise in the dictionary.

For the sake of making the dictionary an easy reference, most flowers are cross-referenced between their common name and botanical name. For example, you will find Hypericum (St. John's Wort) and then also St. John's Wort (Hypericum). The purpose of this dictionary is to use it as a reference for floriography. Please note that there may be flowers and plants entered here that are not botanically accurate. This is a common and ongoing perplexity in horticulture references and language of flowers dictionaries. There are plants and flowers that are perpetually shrouded in confusion as to what genus they belong to and have been that way for many years. I have not attempted to make any corrections in these cases, but I have made effort to clarify them by using their primary Western garden flora terminology, so they are easily identified by the reader.

There are two levels in flower definitions—the primary meaning and then the sub-meaning. The sub-meanings are the ones that have different definitions based on colors or variety. Sometimes the genus will have a specific definition to its variety, which will be listed directly following the name. For example, clematis is a genus, and it has its own primary meaning, but one of its different varieties, such as evergreen, will have additional and different meanings. Another example is geranium, with its primary definitions of comfort, conjugal affection, true friend, peaceful mind, but then, the different *scents* of geranium all have their own additional definitions and different characteristics depending on the shapes of their leaves: silver-edged, pencil-leaf, oak-leaf, etc. Another example is the rose, which has a primary meaning, but then each color has its own meaning as well. As I have stated earlier in the book, you do not have to use all the meanings when you're using the language of flowers to make a posy. Just choose the sentiment that most applies to your message—or several, if it's appropriate.

Abutilon

denotes a new flower entry

A

Abutilon, *Flowering Maple*	meditation, grace, dignity
Abelia	gratitude
Abelia, Glossy	sleekness
Abele, *White Poplar*	time
Abronia, *Sand Verbena*	delicacy, refinement
Absinthe, *Wormwood, Artemisia absinthium*	absence, not to be discouraged, affection, bitterness, comfort, protection for travelers
Acacia	chaste love, friendship, beauty in retirement
Acacia, Rose	elegance, platonic love, friendship
Acacia, yellow-color	secret love, concealed love
Acacia leaves	my heart is buried, affection beyond the grave
Acacia, white-color	friendship, ours is a chaste love
Acanthus, *Bear's Breech*	artifice, the fine arts, unbreakable bonds
Achania malvaviscus, *Wax Mallow, Turk's Cap Mallow*	reserve
Achillea, *Yarrow*	cure for heartache, heals wounds, health sorrow (in war times), to dispel melancholy and heartache
Achimenes, *Magic Flower, Cupid's Bower*	such worth is rare
Aconite, *Anconitum napellis, Helmet Flower, Monkshood, Wolfsbane, Turk's Cap, Friar's Cap*	misanthropy, treachery, poisonous words, symbol of crime, an enemy in disguise, chivalry, knight-errantry
Aconite, Crowfoot	luster
Acorn	Nordic symbol of life and immortality
Adam's Needle, *Yucca*	natural charms, abundant and hardy life
Adder's Tongue Fern	jealousy
Adonis Flos, *Pheasant's Eye*	sorrowful remembrance, painful recollections
Adonis Vernalis	bitter memories
Adlumia, *Allegheny Vine, Climbing Fumitory*	good nature

Aeonium, *Echeveria, Hens and Chicks, Houseleek, Sempervivum, Succulents*	long life, vivacity, domestic economy, welcome home, resilience, robust
Aethusa cynapium, *Fool's Parsley*	silliness
African Daisy, *Cape Marigold, Dimorphotheca*	foreknowledge
African Violet, *Saintpaulia*	faithfulness
Agapanthus, *Lily of the Nile*	love letters, love, enduring spiritual beauty and purity
Agave	tree of life (Mexico), abundance
Ageratum	undying affection, politeness
Agnus castus, *Chaste Tree, Vitex*	coldness, living without love
Agonis, *Burgundy Willow, Peppermint Willow, Willow Myrtle**	grace, poise, versatility, attraction, balance
Agrimony, *Church Steeples, Sticklewort*	gratitude, thankfulness, recognition
Agrostemma, *Corn Cockle*	gentility, peerless and proud
Ajuga, *Bugle*	most loveable, cheers the heart
Alder	protection, symbol of appearance and glamour
Alethea frutex, *Rose of Sharon, Syrian Mallow*	consumed by love, delicate beauty, beautiful, persuasion
Alfalfa, *Lucerne*	life
Allamanda	good disposition, heavenly chief
Allegheny Vine, *Adlumia, Climbing Fumitory*	good nature
Alchemilla mollis, *Lady's Mantle*	comforting love
Allium, *Flowering Onion*	patience, unity, humility
Allspice	compassion
Almond Tree	abiding love and friendship
Almond, flowering	hope, promise, thoughtfulness, lover's charm
Almond	lover's charm, hope, imprudence, stupidity, indiscretion, divination, wisdom, clairvoyance, money, and business
Aloe	grief, sorrow, religious superstition, dejection, affection, botany, overcomes grief, devotion, spiritual and physical healing

Alonsoa, *Mask Flower*	gratitude
Alstromeria, *Peruvian Lily*	friendship, devotion, aspiring, wealth, prosperity, fortune, strength
Alternanthera, *Calico Plant, Joseph's Coat*	favoritism
Althea frutex, *Rose of Sharon, Syrian Mallow*	consumed by love, delicate beauty, beautiful, persuasion
Althea officianalis, *Marsh Mallow*	beneficence, to cure, persuasion, consumed by love, charity, humanity
Alyssum, Sweet	worth beyond beauty, excellence beyond beauty, exemplary modesty, tranquility
Amaranth	immortality, fidelity, everlasting friendship
Amaranth, *Cockscomb*	affectation, foppery, singularity, humor, silliness
Amaranth, Feather, *Celosia*	symbol of affection, unfading love, I blush for you, immortality
Amaranth, Globe	unfading love, constant, unchangeable, immortal or unchangeable love
Amaranth, *Amaranthus caudatus, Hanging Amaranth, Love-lies-bleeding*	desertion, hopeless but not heartless, immortality
Amaranth, Prince's Feather	warmth and caring, I blush for you, unfading love
Amaryllis	pride, splendid beauty, timidity, a coquette, pastoral poetry
Amaryllis Belladonna, *Naked ladies, Belladonna Lily*	pure loveliness, I dream of you, you are a dream
Amazon Lily, *Eucharis Lily*	beauty, maidenly charms
Ambrosia, *Ragweed*	love returned, will you return my love?
American Cowslip	you are my divinity, divine beauty
American Elm, *Ulmus americana*	patriotism, dignity, grace, protection, vigor
American Linden	marital virtues, conjugal love, matrimony
American Starwort	welcome to a stranger, cheerfulness in old age
American Wormseed, *Jerusalem Oak*	your love is reciprocated
Amethyst, *Browallia*	admiration, could you bare poverty?, my love for you is undying
Ammi majus, *Queen Anne's Lace, Bishop's Flower*	haven, sanctuary, protection, warmth, fantasy

Amorpha, *False Indigo*	imperfection
Ampelopsis quinquefolia, *Virginia Creeper, Woodbine, also includes Porcelain Vine*	I cling to you both in sunshine and shade, fraternal love, shyness
Anagallis, *Pimpernel*	change, fickleness
Anchusia, *Bugloss*	falsehood
Anconitum napellis, *Aconite, Helmet Flower, Monkshood, Wolfsbane*	misanthropy, treachery, poisonous words, symbol of crime, an enemy in disguise, chivalry, knight-errantry
Andromeda, *Pieris, Lily of the Valley Shrub*	happy thoughts, happiness through the ages, self-sacrifice
Anemone, *Windflower*	sincerity, truth, abandonment, forsaken, expectation, anticipation, symbol of love
Anemone coronaria, *Garden Anemone*	belief, faith, forsaken, sickness, pain of parting, love's transience
Anemone nemorosa, *Wood Anemone*	anticipation
Anemone nobilis, *Hepatica, Liverwort*	confidence, trust, apathy, your love makes me happy, constancy, permanence
Anemone, *Japanese Wind Flower*	refusal, abandonment
Anemone pulsatilla, *Mayday Flower, Pasque Flower, Wind Anemone*	you have no claims, unpretentious
Anemone, darker shades	the forsaken, sickness, or strength against these things
Angelica	inspiration, magic
Angel's Trumpets, *Brugmansia*	fame, kind thoughts of those dearly departed deceitful charms, disguise, separation
Angrec, *Christmas Orchid, Darwin's Orchid*	royalty, secret love, chaste love
Anigozanthos manglesii, *Kangaroo Paws*	unequal, oblique, distorted
Aniseed	restoration of youth
Anthemis nobilis, *Garden Chamomile*	fortitude, cheerfulness in adversity, patience, comfort, energy in action, endurance, and healing
Anthericum, *Spider Plant*	antidote
Anthurium, *Flamingo Flower, Laceleaf*	the heart, little boy flower, lover, my love

Antirrhinum, *Snapdragon*	strength, gracious lady, power of will, presumpsion, coarseness, incivility, freedom
Antirrhinum, Wild, *Toad Flax*	presumption
Apocynum, *Dogsbane, Indian Hemp*	falsehood, I doubt you, deceit, figment
Apple	healing, prosperity, love, bounty, abundance, perpetual youth, innocence, strength, beauty, temptation, represents a choice
Apple (Chinese tradition)	peace be with you
Apple Blossom	preference, fame speaks great and good of him
Apple Thorn	deceitful charms
Apricot	love
Aquelia, *Columbine*	resolved to win, folly, hypocrisy, I cannot give thee up, gifts of the Holy Spirit, strength, wisdom, salvation
Arabian Jasmine, *Sambac, Indian Jasmine*	attraction, I attach myself to you, attachment, love, fidelity, devotion, dedication
Arborvitae	unchanging friendship live for me, tree of life, old age
Argentina or Argentine, *Silverweed*	naiveté, timidity, simplicity
Arbutus unedo, *Strawberry Tree*	esteem and love
Arbutus, *Madrone, Madrona, Strawberry Tree*	thee only do I love, you are my only love, esteem and love
Arbutus, Trailing, *Ground Laurel, Mayflower*	welcome to a budding beauty, perseverance
Arkansas Coreopsis	love at first sight
Arisaema, *Jack-in-the-Pulpit*	continued happiness, love springs eternal
Armeria, *Thrift, Sea Thrift*	sympathy
Aronia, *Choke Berry*	of value, handy, helpful, effective, favorable
Artemisia, *Silver King*	dignity, power, silver moonlight, sentimental recollections, unceasing remembrance, happiness
Artemisia absinthium, *Absinthe, Wormwood*	absence, not to be discouraged, affection, bitterness, comfort, protection for travelers
Artemisia vulgaris, *Mugwort*	dignity, tranquility, peace, happiness
Arum *Cuckoopint, Arum Lily (hardy), Lords and Ladies*	ardor, ferocity, deceit, zeal
Arum dracontium (green), *Dragon Root*	ardor

Arum, Dragon, *Viagra Lily, Dragonwort*	horror, dread, astonishment
Arum Lily, *Calla Lily, Zantedeschia*	feminine modesty, loveliness, pure elegance, magnificent beauty, with me you are safe, panache
Asclepias, *Butterfly Weed, Milkweed, Swallow-wort*	hope in misery, medicine, cure for heartache, let me go
Ash-Leaved Trumpet Flower, *Bignonia radicans*	separation
Ash, Mountain, *Mountainash Tree, Witchwood Tree*	prudence, purification, protection, with me you are safe, divination, ambition, healing, empowerment, tree of life, treachery
Ash Tree	grandeur, obedience
Asp of Jerusalem, *Dyer's Woad, Isatis tinctorial, Woad*	modest merit
Aspen Tree	lamentation
Asphodel	my regrets will follow you to the grave, memorial sorrow
Asphodel, yellow-color, *Kingspear, Jacob's Rod*	regret
Aster, general	symbol & talisman of love, daintiness, contentment, variety, delicacy, patience, love vibrations, elegance, beauty in retirement, sentimental recollections
Aster, China	variety, fidelity, I will think of it
Aster, double	I share your sentiments
Aster, large-flowered	mental reservations, afterthought
Aster, Monte Cristo	enthusiasm
Aster, *Starwort*	cheerfulness in old age, welcome to a stranger, the star
Aster, Stokes, *Stokesia laevis**	refreshing friendships, extraordinary character, unique and distinquished personality
Aster, Tradescanti, *Michaelmas Daisy, New England Aster, Belgian Aster*	afterthought, memories, farewell, healthy emotions, autumn, love & contentment, variety, delicacy, love vibrations
Aster, single	I will think of it
Aster, wild	drives away evil, sacred star
Astragulus, *Milkvetch*	your presence softens my pain

*Azaleas grow naturally only in dry soil. When offered too much richness from
earth and water, they sicken and decay. Azaleas represent temperance; they grow
and thrive in desolate environments, demonstrating control over their well-being,
which is ultimately representative of a tranquil mind.*

Astrantia, *Masterwort*	strength, power, courage, protection
Astilbe	I'll still be waiting, worldly pleasures
Auricula, *Primula auricula*	painting, pride of newly acquired fortune, wealth is not always happiness
Auricula, green-edged	I'm not important
Auricula, scarlet-color	avarice, pride
Aurinia, *Basket of Gold, Golden Alyssum*	tranquility
Autumn leaves	melancholy
Azalea	first love, love, romance, gratitude, temperance, moderation, take care, fragile, passion, Chinese symbol of womanhood
Azalea, Indian	truth to the end

B

Baby Blue Eyes, *Nemophila menziesii*	success, prosperity, safety, security, open-heartedness
Baby's Breath, *Gypsophilia*	pure heart, festivity, gaiety, everlasting love, innocence, happiness
Bachelor's Button, *Cornflower*	delicacy, felicity, healing properties, single blessedness, celibacy, refinement, devotion, hope, hope in love
Bacon and Eggs Flower, *Birdsfoot Trefoil*	revenge
Balloon Flower, *Platycodon*	return of a friend is desired
Balloon Plant, *Love-in-a-Puff vine**	surprise, charming, sultry, heart, my heart, delicate love

Balm	sympathy, ardent love, impatience, relief from sadness, pleasantry
Balm, Bee, *Monarda, Bergamot*	compassion, sweet virtues, your wiles are irresistible!
Balm, Lemon	healing, fun, humor, love, relief, sharpens wit and understanding, pleasantry, sympathy
Balm of Gilead, *Cottonwood Tree*	relief, cure
Balsam, annual bush	ardent love
Balsam, red-color impatiens	touch me not, impatient resolves
Balsam, yellow-color impatiens	impatience, impatience for love
Balsam of Peru, *Myroxylon*	cure, cure for heartache
Bamboo	loyalty, steadfastness, strength
Banksia, *Grevillea, Leucodendron, Protea*	steadfastness, diversity, loyalty, intent
Barberry	sourness of temper, sharpness, remorse
Basil	best wishes, kingly, royal, betrothal, highly spiritual, luck, hatred, courage
Bouquet of Basil	I am offended
Basket of Gold, *Aurinia, Golden Alyssum*	tranquility
Bassia, *Silver Kochia**	adaptable, rugged for survival, resilient, orderly
Bayberry, *Wax Myrtle*	good luck, instruction, discipline, duty
Bay Leaf (single), *Laurel Leaf (single)*	assured happiness, I change in death, strength
Bay Laurel Wreath	reward of merit
Bay, Sweet, *Laurus nobilis*	famous and notable, triumph of humanity, glory, personal achievement, success, achievement in the arts, reward of merit
Bearded Crepis	protection
Beardtongue, *Penstemon*	spiritual knowledge, understanding
Bear's Breech, *Acanthus*	artifice, the fine arts, unbreakable bonds
Beautyberry, *Callicarpa**	honesty, loyal, respectfulness, good character, integrity
Bee Balm, *Monarda, Bergamot*	compassion, sweet virtues, your wiles are irresistible!

Betony has an unusual flowering characteristic: The flowers bloom in a short spike at the top, then there is stem growth, then another burst of flowers further up the stem. Hence the plant's meaning. . . surprise!

Bee Blossom, *Gaura, Siskiyou Pink, Wand Flower**	refreshing personality, exhilarating, lively, ability, intellect
Bee Orchis, *Early Purple Orchid*	industry
Bee Ophrys, *Bee Orchid*	error
Beech Tree	prosperity, lover's tryst, prosperity, treason, grandeur
Begonia	highly popular, long beautiful, dark thoughts, unrequited love, beware, a fanciful nature, cordiality, patron of science
Begonia, Strawberry	cleverness
Belladonna	silence
Belladonna Lily, *Amaryllis belladonna, Naked Ladies*	pure loveliness, I dream of you, you are a dream
Bellflower, *Campanula*	constancy, aspiring, return of a friend is desired, prairie
Bellflower, *Campanula*, white-color	gratitude
Bells-of-Ireland	whimsy, good luck, gratitude
Bellwort	hopelessness
Bergamot, *Monarda, Bee Balm*	your wiles are irresistible!, compassion, sweet virtues
Bergenia, *Elephant-eared Saxifrage, Elephant's Ears, Pigsqueak**	reliability, steadfastness, robust love, courageous, creative energy, reinvented love
Berzelia*	humility, modesty, sincerity, admiration, I am shy
Belvedere, *Mexican Firebrush, Mock Cypress*	I declare against you
Betony	surprise
Bignonia radicans, *Ash-Leaved Trumpet Flower*	separation
Bindweed, *Convolvulus, Field Bindweed*	bonds, I want your support, dead hope, uncertainty, dangerous insinuation, let us unite

Bindweed, Tricolor, *Convolvulus minor*, *Blue Bindweed*, *Dwarf Morning Glory*	repose, night, obstinacy, humility
Birch	meekness, graciousness, self-sacrifice, devotion, rebirth, protection, purification, new beginnings
Bird of Paradise	joyful, magnificence, a symbol of faithfulness
Bird's-eye Speedwell, *Germander Speedwell*	facility, the more I see you, the more I love you
Birdsfoot Trefoil, *Bacon and Eggs Flower*	revenge
Birthroot, *Trillium*, *Wake Robin*	modest ambition, modest beauty
Bishop's Flower, *Ammi majus*, *Queen Anne's Lace*	haven, sanctuary, prortection, warmth, fantasy
Bittersweet, *Nightshade*	truth, a platonic love, falsehood, silence, dark thoughts, bitter truth, sorcery, spell, witchcraft, skepticism
Blackberry	dangerous pride, envy, jealousy, cares
Black-Eyed (or Brown-Eyed) Susan	justice, impartiality, love conquers all
Black Bryony, *Lady's Seal*	be my support, stay
Black Spider Orchid, *Ophrys*	dexterity
Blackcurrant, *Ribes nigrum*, *Cassis**	happy, ethereal, elation, humor, bliss
Black Poplar	courage
Blackthorn, *Sloe*	difficulty, death, unexpected or sudden change, I have changed radically, insouciance, transition
Bladder Hibiscus, *Flower of an Hour*, *Hibiscus trionum*	delicate beauty, sweet or mild disposition
Bladdernut Tree	frivolity, amusement, idleness
Blanket Flower, *Gaillardia*	aristocratic, vivid, vibrant

Blackthorn, or sloe, means difficulty. Difficulty indeed—have you seen a blackthorn bush and attempted to move around it or touch it? Ouch! It is covered with copious amounts of big thorns!

Bleeding Heart, *Dicentra*	undying love, unrequited love, elegance, fidelity
Bleeding Heart, white-color, *Dicentra*	purity, innocence
Blue Chalk Sticks, *Senecio succulent species*, *String of Bananas*, *String of Pearls**	companionship, harmony, understanding, engaging conversations, curiosity, occasionally spicy personality
Blue-flowered Greek Valerian, *Jacob's Ladder*	rupture, split, come down, grace and elegance, wealth
Blue Shrimp Plant, *Cerinthe, Honeywort, Pride of Gibraltar**	tenacity, constancy, enduring, timeless affection
Blue Vervain, *Volkamenia*	may you be happy
Bluebeard, *Caryopteris**	inventive, gifted, avant-garde, rigor
Bluebell, English and Spanish	constancy, humility, gratitude, occasionally grief
Blueberry, flowers and fruit	healing, prayer, protection
Blueberry, foliage	treachery
Bluebottle, *Centaury*	delicacy, felicity, happiness
Bluets, *Quaker Ladies*	contentment
Bolete Mushroom, *Champignon*	suspicion
Bonus-henricus, *Poor Man's Asparagus, Good-King-Henry*	benevolence, goodness
Borage	bluntness, courage, brusqueness, speak your mind
Boronia	sweetness, lively personality, softens the heart
Bottle Brush, *Callistemon**	abundance, laughter, joy, birth, new and sustaining life
Bottle Rocket, *Leopard Plant, Ligularia**	industrious, useful
Bougainvillea	a beauty, beautiful day, paper, paper flowers
Bouvardia	enthusiasm
Box	stoicism, constancy, ancientness, constancy in friendship
Bramble	lowliness, envy, remorse
Branch of Currants	you please all
Branch of Thorns	severity, rigor
Breath of Heaven, *Coleonema, Confetti Bush, Diosma*	your simple elegance charms me

Briars	envy
Bridal Rose	happy love
Brodiaea, *Cluster-lilies, Fool's Onion**	cultured, intellect, heartfelt, poetic, creative soul, inspired minds
Broom, *Genista*	humility, safety, neatness, cleanliness
Broom, prickly	misanthropy
Browallia, *Amethyst*	admiration, my love for you is undying
Brugmansia, *Angel's Trumpets*	fame, kind thoughts of those dearly departed, deceitful charms, disguise, separation
Bryony, Black, *Lady's Seal*	be my support, stay
Bryony, White	prosperity, support
Buckbean	calm repose
Buckwheat flowers	lover
Buds	promise of good things to come
Bud of White Rose	heart ignorant of love
Buddleia, *Butterfly Bush*	rashness, wantonness
Bugle, *Ajuga*	most loveable, cheers the heart
Bugloss, *Anchusia*	falsehood
Bulrush	indiscretion, docile and gentle
Bundle of Reeds, with their panicles	music
Burdock	importunity, touch me not
Burgundy Willow, *Agonis, Peppermint Willow, Willow Myrtle**	grace, poise, versatility, attraction, balance
Bush Monkey Flower, *Sticky Monkey Flower, Diplacus**	I'm stuck on you, tenacious affection, let's stick together, prevalent fondness, universal love
Buttercup	cheerfulness, ingratitude, childishness, rich in charms
Buttercup, Fig, *Lesser Celandine*	joys to come, future joy, first sigh of love
Butterfly Bush, *Buddleia*	rashness, wantonness
Butterfly Weed, *Asclepias, Milkweed, Swallow-wort*	hope in misery, medicine, cure for heartache, let me go
Buttonbush, *Cephalanthus occidentalis, Button Willow**	victorious, cherished friendship, excels in beauty

C

Cabbage	profit
Cacalia, *Indian Plantain*	adulation, adoration
Cactus	warmth, maternal love, endurance, my heart burns with love, grandeur, enduring love, bravery, endurance
Cactus, Creeping	horror
Caladium	delight, great joy
Calendula, *Pot Marigold*	health, joy, remembrance, constancy, the sun, affection, disquietude, grief, jealousy, misery, cares, constancy, presage, overcomes trouble
Calico Bush, *Mountain Laurel, Kalmia latifolia*	ambition
Calico Plant, *Alternanthera, Joseph's Coat*	favoritism
California Pepper Tree, *Schinus*	religious enthusiasm, sweetness, beauty, wit
Calla Lily, *Arum Lily, Zantadeschia*	feminine modesty, loveliness, pure elegance, magnificent beauty, with me you are safe, panache
Callistemon, *Bottle Brush**	abundance, laughter, joy, birth, new and sustaining life
Callicarpa, *Beautyberry**	honesty, loyal, respectfulness, good character, integrity
Calceolaria, *Lady's Purse, Pocketbook Flower, Slipper Flower*	keep this for my sake
Calycanthus, *Sweetshrub, Carolina Allspice*	benevolence
Calcynia, *Thryptomene, Baeckea imbricata and grandiflora, Grampiens Heath Myrtle, Calynia, Heath Myrtle**	sustenance, adversity, opulence, abundance
Camellia	beauty, excellence, contentment, loveliness, gratitude, pity
Camellia, pink-color	longing, longing for you
Camellia, red-color	unpretending excellence, alas my poor heart, you're a flame in my heart, innate warmth, loveliness

Camellia, white-color	perfected loveliness, adoration, you are adorable, without blemish
Campanula, *Bellflower*	constancy, aspiring, return of a friend is desired, prairie
Campanula, *Bellflower*, white-color	gratitude
Campanula, *Canterbury Bells*	acknowledgment, gratitude
Campanula rotundifolia, *Common Harebell, Lady's Thimble*	submission, grief, humility
Campion, *Lychnis, Catchfly, Jerusalem or Maltese Cross*	snare, religious enthusiasm, sweetness, beauty, wit, sorrows, voyages, sun-beam'd eyes, unchanging friendship, pretended love
Campsis radicans, *Trumpet Flower, Trumpet Vine*	fame
Canariensis, *Date Palm, Pineapple Palm*	self-esteem
Canary Grass	perseverance, determination
Candy Kisses, *Hemizygia, Wild Sage**	cheerful, tenderness, sparkling personality, light-hearted, lively
Candytuft, *Iberis*	sweetness, stoic beauty, indifference, wedding flower
Canna	glorious, magnificent beauty
Canterbury Bells, *Campanula*	acknowledgment, gratitude
Cape Jasmine, *Gardenia*	ecstasy, feminine charm, transport of joy, I'm too happy, you're lovely, secret love, refinement
Cape Marigold, *African Daisy, Dimorphotheca*	foreknowledge
Caraway	infidelity prevented
Cardamine, *Cuckoo Flower Lady's Smock, Meadow Cress*	paternal error, ardor, parental ardor, wit
Cardinal Flower, *Scarlet Lobelia*	distinction

Campanula

Did you know? Carnations, dianthus, wallflower, and stock are all known as the gillyflower!

Carnation	fascination, admiration, ardent and pure love, bonds of love, unfading beauty, woman's love, health and energy, yes, classic symbol of love and affection
Carnation (Spanish tradition)	divine flower for strength, protection and healing
Carnation, laced	passion
Carnation, white-color	good luck, pure and ardent love, sweet and lovely, innocence, faithfulness, women's good luck gift
Carnation, red-color	passion, alas! for my poor heart, deep pure love
Carnation, pink-color	I will always remember you, maternal love, lively and pure affection, beauty, pride, women's love
Carnation, hot pink–color	ardent love
Carnation, purple-color	capriciousness, changeable, whimsical
Carnation, yellow-color	disdain, rejection, disappointment
Carnation, striped	refusal, sorry I cannot be with you, wish I could be with you
Carolina Allspice, *Calycanthus*, *Sweetshrub*	benevolence
Carolina Silverbell, *Helesia Carolina*, *Silverbell Tree**	surprise, epiphany, contentment, good fortune, prosperity, wonderment
Caryopteris, Bluebeard	acknowledgment, inventive, gifted, avant-garde, rigor, delightful presence
Cassia, *fistula*, *Golden Rain Tree*, *Golden Shower Tree*	ray of sunshine, promise, health, healing, radiance, world tree and tree of life (Chinese tradition)
Catalpa	beware of the coquette
Catchfly, *Lychnis*, *Campion*, *Jerusalem or Maltese Cross*	snare, religious enthusiasm, sweetness, beauty, wit, sorrows, voyages, sun-beam'd eyes, unchanging friendship, pretended love
Catchfly, *Lychnis*, *Silene*, red-color	youthful love, sun-beamed eyes

Catchfly, white-color	betrayed, I fall a victim
Cathedral Bells Vine, *Cobaea, Cup and Saucer Vine*	exciting news, gossip, knots or bonds of love
Catmint, *Nepeta mussinii**	mischievous, good-natured, spirited, whimsical, I want to have fun!
Cattail	peace, prosperity
Ceanothus, *Wild Lilac**	reliability, rarity, constancy, vibrant personality
Cedar	strength, prosperity, longevity, long life, drives away negative energies, think of me, I live for thee, majesty
Cedar of Lebanon	incorruptible
Cedar Sprig	constancy in love, I live for thee
Celandine, Lesser, *Fig Buttercup*	joys to come, future joy, first sigh of love
Celosia, *Feather Amaranth*	symbol of affection, unfading love, I blush for you, immortality
Centaury, *Bluebottle*	delicacy, felicity, happiness
Cerasium, *Mouse-ear Chickweed*	simplicity
Cercis Tree, *Judas Tree, Redbud Tree*	love tree, unbelief, sometimes betrayal
Cereus, Creeping, *Night-blooming Cactus*	modest genius, transient beauty, a spectacular moment, radiant, sweet beauty
Cerinthe, *Blue Shrimp Plant, Honeywort, Pride of Gibraltar**	tenacity, constancy, enduring, timeless affection
Chaenomeles, *Japanese Quince, japonica*	symbolic of luck, prosperity, good fortune, love, sincerity
Cestrum, *Night-blooming Jasmine*	transient beauty
Cetraria, *Iceland Moss*	health
Chamelancium, *Geraldton Wax Flower, Stirling Range Wax Flower, Wax Flower*	riches, wealth, lasting love, patience, happy marriage
Chamomile, Garden, *Anthemis nobilis*	fortitude, cheerfulness in adversity, patience, comfort, energy in action, endurance, healing
Champignon, *Bolete Mushroom*	suspicion
Chaste Tree, *Agnus castus, Vitex*	coldness, to live without love
Cheesewood, *Pittosporum**	deviate from difficulties, conquer, shelter, to bring certainty, comfort, blessings

Chelone, *Turtlehead*	pleasure without alloy
Cherry Blossom (Japanese tradition)	transience of life
Cherry Blossom (Chinese tradition)	feminine beauty
Cherry Plum, *Myrobalan Plum*	privation
Cherry Tree	a good education, sweetness of character derived from good works, insincerity
Cherry Tree, white color blooms	deception
Cherry, flowering	chivalry, nobility, spiritual beauty, education, endurance, celebration of new beginnings
Chervil, *Sweet Cicely, Myrrh*	sincerity, gladness
Chestnut, blossom	please do me justice
Chestnut Tree, Horse	luxury, genius
Chichorium, *Succory, Chicory*	frugality, economy
Chickweed	rendezvous, I cling to thee, ingenuous simplicity, give an account for yourself
Chinaberry, *Melia azedarach, Persian Lilac, Pride of India*	dissension, rebellion
China Pink, *Dianthus chinensis, Indian Pink*	aversion
Chinese Fringe Flower, *Loropetalum*★	fun and flirty, witty, merriment, joyful
Chinese Lanterns, *Winter Cherry, Withania somnifera*	deception
Chives, Garlic	courage, protection, strength
Christmas Orchid, *Angrec, Darwin's Orchid*	royalty, secret love, chaste love
Christmas Rose, *Hellebores, Lenten Rose*	relieve my anxiety, protection against calumny, scandal, a beautiful year ahead, wit
Choke Berry, *Aronia*	of value, handy, helpful, effective, favorable
Chrysanthemum	cheerfulness, long life, optimism, love, classic love flower, abundance and wealth, you're a wonderful friend, joy, truth, rest, cheerfulness under adversity, difficulty

Chrysanthemum (European tradition)	symbol of condolence used at funerals and on graves
Chrysanthemum (Japanese tradition)	symbol of the emperor, the sun, lucky golden flowers
Chrysanthemum (Chinese tradition)	loveliness and cheerfulness, cheerfulness in adversity
Chrysanthemum, bronze-color	happy hearth and home, joy, long life, truth, friendship
Chrysanthemum, red-color	love, a classic love symbol
Chrysanthemum, white-color	truth, hope, loyal love, pure and true affections
Chrysanthemum, yellow-color	cheerfulness, sometimes slighted love
Church Steeples, *Agrimony, Sticklewort*	gratitude, thankfulness, recognition
Cinaria	ever bright, always delighted, you are my delight
Cinnamon	beauty, love, forgiveness of injuries, my fortune is yours!
Cinquefoil, *Potentilla*	maternal affection, beloved daughter, beloved child
Circaea, *Enchanter's Nightshade*	fascination, witchcraft
Cistus, *Helianthemum, Rock Rose*	popular favor, security, safety
Cistus, Gum	I shall die tomorrow
Citron	beauty with ill humor, ill-natured beauty
Citronella	sadness, protection, cleansing, man's love, healing
Clarkia	will you dance with me, your witty conversation delights me
Cleavers, *Clotbur*	rudeness
Clematis	mental beauty, ingenuity, unchanged for eternity, artifice, love of family (sons and daughters)
Clematis, evergreen	ingenuity, poverty overcome through mental ingenuity
Clematis, *Virgin's Bower*	love of brother, sister, sons, or daughters
Clematis vitalba, *Traveler's Joy*	rest, safety
Cleome, *Spider Flower*	elope with me, not so bad as I seem
Clethra, *Sweet Pepperbush, Summer Sweet**	generous, favorable, brave, talented
Clianthus, *Parrot's Bill*	self-seeking, worldliness

Climbing Fumitory, *Adlumia, Allegheny Vine*	good nature
Clivia, *Clive, Winter Lily**	you enhance my life, an ornament of beauty and distinction
Clotbur, *Cleavers*	rudeness
Clover	good education, good luck, hard work
Clover, Four-leaf, oxalis acetosella, trifolium repens	faith, hope, luck, love; when given to another: luck be with you, be mine; when given to a lover: you belong to each other
Clover, red or purple	industry, provident
Clover, Three leaf	the Trinity
Clover, white-color	think of me, luck, I promise
Cloves	dignity
Cobaea, *Cathedral Bells Vine, Cup and Saucer Vine*	exciting news, gossip, knots or bonds of love
Cocklebur, *Xanthium*	pertinacity, rudeness
Cockscomb, *Amaranth*	affectation, foppery, singularity, humor, silliness
Coconut Palm	tropical tree of life and abundance
Coeloglossum, *Frog Orchid*	disgust
Colchicum, *Meadow Saffron*	my best days are past
Coleonema, *Breath of Heaven, Confetti Bush, Diosma*	your simple elegance charms me
Coleus*	intensity, excitement, energy, showy
Coltsfoot, *Tussilago*	justice
Columbine, *Aquelia*	resolved to win, folly, hypocrisy, I cannot give thee up, gifts of the Holy Spirit, strength, wisdom, salvation
Columbine, yellow-color	lightness, happiness, vivaciousness, vitality
Columbine, purple-color	penance, resolved to win
Columbine, red-color	anxious, worried
Comfrey	home sweet home
Compass Flower, *Silphium*	faith
Coneflower, purple-color, *Echinacea*	capability, skill, strength, health
Coneflower, yellow- or golden-color, *Echinacea*	justice, impartiality, strength

Confetti Bush, *Breath of Heaven, Coleonema, Diosma*	your simple elegance charms me
Convolvulus, *Field Bindweed*	bonds, I want your support, dead hope, uncertainty, dangerous insinuation, let us unite
Convolvulus major, ipomaea purpurea , *Morning Glory*	extinguished hopes, affection, bonds of love, departure, greet the new day, busybody, coquetry
Convolvulus, pink-color	worth sustained by judicious and tender affection
Convolvulus minor, *Dwarf Morning Glory, Tricolor Bindweed, Blue Bindweed*	repose, night, obstinacy, humility
Coral Bells, *Heuchera*	challenge, hard work
Coral Pea, *Happy Wanderer, Hardenbergia, Vine Lilac**	spirited, happiness, capability, ingenuity
Coral Vine, *Kennedia*	mental beauty, intellectual beauty
Corchorus, *Jute Mallow*	impatient for happiness, absence, return quickly
Cordyline, *Hawaiian Ti Plant, Good Luck Plant, Palm Lily*	majesty, honor, purity of heart
Coreopsis	always cheerful, love at first sight
Coreopsis, Arkansas	love at first sight
Coriander	hidden worth, occasionally lust
Corn, *Maize*	riches, gift of mother earth
Corn, blossom, tassel, or silks	riches, I wish riches for you, I am rich
Corn, broken	quarrel
Corn, bottle	delicacy
Corn Cockle, *Agrostemma*	gentility, peerless and proud
Corn Straw	agreement
Cornel Tree, *Dogwood*	faithfulness, duration, durability, charm, finesse
Cornflower, *Bachelor's Button*	delicacy, felicity, healing properties, single blessedness, celibacy, refinement, devotion, hope, hope in love
Coronilla, *Crown Vetch*	success crowned you
Cornus, *Cornelian Cherry Dogwood*	charm, finesse, durability, I admire your personality
Corydalis, *Fumitory, Fumewort*	practice, gall, the spleen, sometimes anger

Cosmos	modesty, pure love of a virgin, innocent beauty, universal love around the world, love flower, I love you more than anyone can
Cosmos, white-color	joy in love and life
Cosmos, Chocolate*	simple pleasures, the deepest love for you
Cotoneaster*	artful, fun in abundance, highly popular, sometimes bequiling
Cotton*	well-being, gratitude, receiving of a blessing, give and take, fortune
Cottonwood Tree, *Balm of Gilead*	relief, cure
Cowslip	pensiveness, winning grace
Cowslip, American, *Dodecatheon*	divine beauty, you are my divinity
Crabapple, blossom	overcomes irritability, ill-tempered, charming, bewitching, mild
Cranberry	cure for heartache
Cranesbill, *Crowsbill, Hardy Geranium*	constancy, availability, I desire to please, envy, wishes come true, imbecility, steadfast piety
Crassula, *Grammanthes*	your temper is too hasty
Crassula ovata, *Jade Plant/Tree*	symbol of good fortune, wealth, health, happiness
Creeping Jenny, *Lysmachia*	forgiveness, womb plant
Crepe Myrtle, *Lagerstromia*	eloquence
Cress	stability, power, resolution
Crinum, large-flowering	lovely, proud of spirit, majesty, delicate beauty
Crinum, small-flowering	refined and delicate beauty, tenderness, weakness
Crocus	pleasure of hope, youthful gladness, cheerfulness, abuse not, joy
Crocus, Saffron	mirth, gladness, gaiety
Crocus, Autumn	thankful, good cheer as our finest days are passing
Crocus, Spring	joy and youthful gladness
Crown Imperial, *Fritillaria, Imperial Lily*	majesty, power, pride of birth, arrogance
Crowfoot, Marsh	ingratitude
Crowfoot, Aconite-leaved	luster
Crown Vetch, *Coronilla*	success crowned you

Crowsbill, *Cranesbill, Hardy Geranium*	constancy, availability, I desire to please, envy, wishes come true, imbecility, steadfast piety
Cuckoo Flower, *Cardamine, Lady's Smock, Meadow Cress*	paternal error, ardor, parental ardor, wit
Cuckoopint, *Arum, Lords and Ladies, Arum Lily (hardy)*	*ardor, zeal, ferocity, deceit*
Cucumber	criticism
Cudweed, American	unceasing remembrance
Cup and Saucer Vine, *Cathedral Bells Vine, Cobaea*	exciting news, gossip, knots or bonds of love
Cupid's Bower, *Achimenes, Magic Flower*	such worth is rare
Currant, Black, *Ribes nigrum, Blackcurrant, Cassis**	happy, ethereal, elation, humor, bliss
Currant, *Ribes*	thy frown will kill me
Currants, bunch of	you please all!
Cuscuta, *Dodder, Dodder of Thyme*	baseness, bad character, meanness
Cyclamen	diffidence, resignation and good-bye, I am shy, timidity, lacking self-confidence
Cypress	death, mourning, despair, grief, eternal sorrow
Cypress Vine, *Quamoclit*	busybody, curiosity

D

Daffodil, common *Narcissus*	regard, respect, unrequited love, sunshine, the sun shines when I am with you, chivalry, you're the only one
Daffodil, gift of a single flower	you are the only love, unrequited love
Daffodil, bunches or several	joy, happiness, celebration
Daffodil, *Paperwhite Narcissus*	self-esteem, hope, prosperity, renewal, gracefulness, respect, self-love, national flower of Wales, aphrodisiac, sweetness, you are sweet
Daffodil, Naturalized Wild, *Lent Lily*	sweet disposition
Dahlia	dignity, eloquence, gratitude, instability
Dahlia bouquet	my gratitude surpasses your cares
Dahlia, double	participation

Dahlia, single	good taste
Dahlia, variegated	I think of you constantly!
Dahlia, white-color	gratitude to parents
Dahlia, yellow-color	I am happy that you love me
Daisy, field	innocence, simplicity, patience, sadness
Daisy, colored	beauty
Daisy, double	affection, participation, I share your sentiments
Daisy, English	innocence, simplicity, purity, newborn, cheer, popular oracle, I share your sentiments
Daisy, Everlasting, *Eternal Flower, Xeranthemum*	unfading remembrance, cheerful in adversity, eternity, and immortality
Daisy Fleabane, *Santa Barbara Daisy*	thank you
Daisy, Gerbera	friendship, sadness, needing protection, innocence, purity
Daisy, Rudbeckia	justice, impartiality
Daisy, red-color	beauty unknown to possessor
Daisy, Marguerite	variety, oracle of the meadows
Daisy, Michaelmas, *New England Aster, Belgian Aster*	afterthought, memories, farewell, healthy emotions, autumn, cheerfulness in old age
Daisy, Ox-eyed	patience, be patient, attracts wealth, obstacle, token of affection
Dame's Rocket, *Queen's Rocket, Sweet Rocket, Hesperis matronalis*	fashionable, you are the queen of coquettes!, evening, evening star, danger, rivalry
Dame's Rocket, white-color	despair not
Damson Tree	independence
Dandelion	wishes granted, faithful and happy, love's oracle
Daphne	painting the lily (adorn something already beautiful), desire to please, fame, glory, coquetry
Daphne, February, *Mezereum*	desire to please, a flirt
Darling Pea, *Swainsona**	bold yet graceful, a lady in every way, resilient, graceful beauty, consistently beautiful
Darwin's Orchid, *Angrec, Christmas Orchid*	royalty, secret love, chaste love
Datura, *Moon Flower, Jimsonweed, Thornapple*	delusive beauty, disguise, deceitful charms

Datura, Black, *Datura fastuosa, Datura Metel, Devil's Trumpet, Double Purple Thornberry*	suspicion
Day Lily, *Hemerocallis*	wealth and pride, success, flirty
Day Lily, *Hemerocallis* (Chinese tradition)	emblem of the mother
Dead Leaves	sadness, melancholy
Deadly Nightshade	falsehood
Delphinium	sweetness, well-being, big-hearted, fun, lightness, heavenly, levity, airy
Deutzia*	delicate and ample beauty, exuberant grace, lavish, charm, elegance
Devil's Trumpet, *Black Datura, Datura fastuosa, Datura Metel, Double Purple Thornberry*	suspicion
Dew Plant, *Ice Plant, Ficoides, Fig Marigold*	serenade, old beau, rejected, cold-hearted, your looks freeze me, idleness, rejected addresses
Dianthus barbatus, *Pink, Sweet William*	love, affection, boldness, pure affection, classic love flower, childhood, memory, grant me one smile, perfection, finesse
Dianthus chinensis, *China Pink, Indian Pink*	aversion
Dicentra, *Bleeding Heart*	undying love, unrequited love, elegance, fidelity
Dicentra, *Bleeding Heart* white-color	purity, innocence
Digitalis, *Foxglove*	stately, youth, insincerity
Dill	soothing
Dimorphotheca, *African Daisy, Cape Marigold*	foreknowledge
Diosma, *Coleonema, Breath of Heaven, Confetti Bush*	your simple elegance charms me
Diplacus, *Bush Monkey Flower, Sticky Monkey Flower**	I'm stuck on you, tenacious affection, let's stick together, prevalent fondness, universal love
Dipscaus, *Teasel*	misanthropy
Dittany of Crete, *Hop Marjoram*	birth, childbirth
Dittany of Crete, white	passion

Dock	patience
Dodder, or Dodder of Thyme, *Cuscuta*	baseness, bad character, meanness
Dodecatheon, *American Cowslip*	divine beauty, you are my divinity
Dodonaea viscosa, *Hopseed Bush**	abundance in creativity, highly adaptable, impervious to adversity
Dog Rose	pleasure and pain
Dogsbane, *Apocynum, Indian Hemp*	falsehood, I doubt you, deceit, figment
Dogwood, *Cornel Tree*	faithfulness, duration, durability, charm, finesse, I am perfectly indifferent to you
Dogwood, flowering	I admire your personality and social abilities, our love will endure adversity
Dogwood, *Red-Osier, Redosier Dogwood*	frankness
Double Purple Thornberry, *Black Datura, Datura fastuosa, Datura Metel, Devil's Trumpet*	suspicion
Dragon Plant, *Dracaena marginata*	snare
Dragon Root, *Arum dracontium (green)*	ardor
Dragonwort, *Dragon Arum, Viagra Lily*	horror, dread, astonishment
Dried Flax	utility
Drosera, *Round-leafed Sundew*	surprise
Dusty Miller	felicity, delicacy, venerable, industriousness
Dyer's Woad, *Asp of Jerusalem, Isatis tinctorial, Woad*	modest merit

E

Ebony Tree	blackness, darkness, suppleness, grace, hyposcrisy
Echeveria, *Aeonium, Hens and Chicks, Houseleek, Sempervivum, Succulents*	long life, vivacity, domestic economy, welcome home, resilience, robust
Echinacea, *Purple Coneflower*	capability, skill, strength, health
Echinacea, yellow or gold color, *Coneflower*	justice, impartiality, strength

Edelweiss	courage, devotion
Eglantine, *Rosa rubiginosa, Sweet Briar, European*	I wound to heal, a poetic person, poetry
Elder	zealousness, compassion
Elderberry, *Sambucus*	compassion, kindness
Elecampane, *Horseheal, Elfdock*	tears
Elm, American, *Ulmus*	dignity, grace, protection, patriotism, vigor
Enchanter's Nightshade, *Circaea*	fascination, witchcraft
Endive	frugality
Epilobium, *Rosebay Willow Herb*	production, celibacy
Equisetum, *Horsetail Rush*	docility
Eriostemon, *Philotheca* *	my beloved, dear to me, loved
Eryngium, *Sea Holly*	attraction
Escallonia*	pillar of strength, protection, security, creativity, artistic endeavor
Eschscholtzia, *California Poppy*	sweetness
Eternal Flower, *Everlasting Daisy, Xeranthemum*	unfading remembrance, cheerful in adversity, eternity, and immortality
Eucalyptus	protection, healing
Eucomis, *Pineapple Lily* *	epiphany, prideful, majestic, abundance, but can also mean deceptive charm
Euonymus, *Spindle Tree*	long life, your image is engraved on my heart
Eupatorium, *Joe Pye Weed*	delay, love, respect
Euphorbia, *Spurge*	purification, protection, persistence, welcome
Evening Primrose, *Oenothera, Sun Cups, Sun Drops*	happiness, happy love, sometimes inconstancy, mildness
Evergreen	poverty
Evergreen Thorn	solace in adversity
Everlasting, *Immortelle, Helichrysum italicum*	never-ceasing memory, perpetual remembrance, endless love
Everlasting Pea	lasting pleasure, an appointed meeting
Eyebright, *Monkeyflower, Musk-Plant*	be bolder, weakness

F

False Indigo, *Amorpha*	imperfection
Fennel	force, strength, worthy of praise
Fern	fascination, sincerity, magic, shelter
Fern, *Leatherleaf*	fascination, fidelity, I promise to be true, discretion
Fern, Maidenhair	secret bond of love, discretion
Fern, Royal and Cinnamon, *Osmunda*	reverie, I dream of thee
Feverfew (and hybrids), *Tanacitum*	good health, warmth, you light up my life, protection
Fever Root	delay
Ficoides, *Dew Plant*, *Ice Plant*, *Fig Marigold*	serenade, old beau, rejected, cold-hearted, your looks freeze me, idleness, rejected addresses
Fig	longevity, peace, prosperity, strength, energy, prolific
Filbert	reconciliation
Filipendula rubra, *Queen of the Prairie*	farsighted outlook
Fir Tree	time, height, cleverness, adaptability, ability to change, spirit of the forest
Fir, foliage	adaptability, elevation, will, desire, all-seeing
Fistula, *Golden Rain Tree*, *Golden Shower Tree*, *Cassia*	ray of sunshine, promise, health, healing, radiance, world tree and tree of life (Chinese tradition)
Flax	domestic symbol, industry, fate, I feel your kindness
Flax, dried	utility
Flax, New Zealand	tenacity, holding fast, basket, wickerwork
Flax-leaved Goldilocks, *Goldilocks Aster*	tardiness, you're late!
Fleur-de-lis, *Iris*	ardor, faith, eloquence, wisdom, promise in love, hope, valor, valued friendship, message, emblem of France, I burn with passion
Floradora, *Stephanotis*	wedding, marital happiness, desire to travel

Fern

Flowering Moss, *Pyxie*	life is sweet
Flowering Reed	confidence in heaven
Flower-of-an-hour, *Hibiscus trionum*, *Bladder Hibiscus*	delicate beauty, tropical love, consumed by love, sweet or mild disposition
Flowering Maple, *Abutilon*	meditation, grace, dignity
Flowering Onion, *Allium*	patience, unity, humility
Fly Trap, Venus	deceit, caught at last, duplicity
Fool's Parsley, *Aethusa cynapium*	silliness
Fool's Onion, *Brodiaea*, *Cluster-lilies**	cultured, intellect, heartfelt, poetic, creative soul, inspired minds
Forget-Me-Not	hope, remembrance, true love
Forsythia	good nature, anticipation
Forsythia (Chinese tradition)	symbol of luck, prosperity, good fortune, love
Four-leaf Clover, *oxalis acetosella*, *trifolium repens*	faith, hope, luck, love; when given to another: luck be with you, be mine; when given to a lover: you belong to each other
Four O'Clock	the chameleon, timidity, evening beauty, sweet dreams
Foxglove, *Digitalis*	stateliness, youth, insincerity, young manliness, youth, a wish, decision, I am not ambitious for myself, but for you
Foxtail Grass	sporting
Frankincense	a faithful heart
Fraxinella, *Gas Plant*	fire
Freesia	innocence, trust, thoughtfulness
French Honeysuckle	rustic beauty
French Marigold	comforts the heart, jealousy, overcomes jealousy
Fritillaria, *Imperial Lily*, *Crown Imperial*	majesty, power, pride of birth, arrogance
Fritillaria, chequered, *Snakes Head*	persecution
Frog Orchid, *Coeloglossum*	disgust
Fuschsia	humble love, good taste, confiding love
Fuschsia, Scarlet	will you confide in love, delicate charms, taste, the ambition in my love thus plagues itself

Fuller's Teasel	misanthropy, importunity
Fumitory, *Corydalis, Fumewort*	practice, gall, the spleen, sometimes anger
Furze, *Gorse, Whin*	enduring affection, love for all occasions, can also mean anger

G

Gaillardia, *Blanket Flower*	aristocratic, vivid, vibrant
Galanthus, *Snowdrop*	hope, friendship, support, consolation, refinement, a friend in adversity
Galax	encouragement, friendship
Galega, *Goat's Rue*	reason
Galium, *Sweet Woodruff*	humility, patience
Garden Chervil, *Sweet Cicely, Myrrh*	sincerity, gladness
Gardenia, *Cape Jasmine*	ecstasy, feminine charm, transport of joy, I'm too happy, you're lovely, secret love, refinement
Garland of Roses	reward of virtue
Garlic	protection, strength, get well, courage, ward off evil and illness, good luck
Garlic Chives	courage, protection, strength
Gas Plant, *Fraxinella*	fire
Gaultheria shallon, *Salal*	zest, divine healing
Gaura, *Bee Blossom, Siskiyou Pink, Wand Flower**	refreshing personality, exhilarating, lively, ability, intellect
Gay-Feather, *Liatris*	gaiety
Genista, *Broom*	humility, safety, neatness, cleanliness
Gentian	you are unjust, loveliness, righteousness, integrity
Gentian, fringed	intrinsic worth, I look to heaven, autumn
Gentian, closed	sweet be thy dreams
Gentian, yellow-color	ingratitude
Geraldton Wax Flower, *Stirling Range Wax Flower, Chamelancium, Wax Flower*	riches, wealth, lasting love, patience, happy marriage
Geranium, general, *Pelargoniums*	comfort, conjugal affection, true friend, peaceful mind

Geranium, dark-leafed	you are childish!, melancholy, deceit, stupidity, childhood
Geranium, apple-scented	present preference, facility
Geranium, Ivy	bridal favor, I engage you for the next dance
Geranium, Lemon-scented	unexpected meeting
Geranium, Nutmeg-scented	expected meeting
Geranium, Oak-leaf	true friendship, lady, deign to smile
Geranium, penciled or skeleton	ingenuity
Geranium, rose-scented	preference, I prefer you
Geranium, scented	comfort, gentility, preference
Geranium, silver-leaf (Pelargonium sidoides)	recall, admiration
Geranium, pink-color	gentility
Geranium, peppermint-scented	invigoration, inspiration, healing
Geranium, red-color	comfort, health, protection, folly, stupidity, preference
Geranium, white-color	gracefulness
Geranium, hardy or wild, *Cranesbill, Crowsbill*	constancy, availability, I desire to please, envy, wishes come true, imbecility, steadfast piety
Germander Speedwell, *Bird's-eye Speedwell*	facility, the more I see you, the more I love you
Geum*	cheerful, delightful, future is waiting with open arms
Gillyflower, *Stock*	lasting beauty, promptness, bonds of affection, happy life, you'll always be beautiful to me
Gillyflower, *Wallflower*	lasting beauty, fidelity in aversity, promptness, luxury
Ginger	pleasant, safe, warming, comfort
Ginkgo biloba, *Maidenhair Tree**	longevity, solitary beauty, enlightenment, profound endurance
Gladiolus	generosity, strength of character, love at first sight, splendid beauty, admiration, give me a break, remembrance, I am sincere
Gladiolus acidanthera, *Peacock Orchid*	distinction

Globe Amaranth	unfading love, constant, unchangeable, immortal or unchangable love
Globe Flower, *Trollius*	solitude, generosity, gratitude
Gloriosa Lily, *Gloriosa superba*	union of the lover and the beloved
Glory Flower, *Tibouchina urvilleana*, *Princess Flower*	glorious beauty, glory protection against cruelty, occasionally cruelty, for once may pride befriend me!
Gloxinia	a proud spirit, love at first sight
Goat's Rue, *Galega*	reason
Gourd	extent, bulk, support, prosperity
Godetia, *Satin Flower*	fascination, sincerity, love flower
Golden Alyssum, *Aurinia, Basket of Gold*	tranquility
Golden Chain Tree, *Laburnum*	forsaken, pensive beauty
Golden Rain Tree, *fistula, Golden Shower Tree, Cassia*	ray of sunshine, promise, health, healing, radiance, world tree and tree of life (Chinese tradition)
Goldenrod, *Solidago, Solidaster*	encouragement, precaution, good fortune, protection
Goldilocks Aster, *Flax-leaved Goldilocks*	tardiness, you're late!
Good-King-Henry, *Bonus-henricus, Poor Man's Asparagus*	benevolence, goodness
Good Luck Plant, *Cordyline, Palm Lily, Hawaiian Ti Plant*	majesty, honor, purity of heart
Gooseberry	anticipation
Goosefoot	goodness, occasional insult
Gorse, *Furze, Whin*	enduring affection, love for all occasions, can also mean anger
Grammanthes, *Crassula*	your temper is too short
Grampians Heath Myrtle, *Thryptomene, Calcynia, Calynia, Heath Myrtle, Baeckea imbricata and grandiflora, Kardomia**	sustenance, diversity, opulence, abundance
Grape	domestication, hospitality, charity, intemperance
Grape, vines	intoxication, bonds, intemperance
Grape, wild	charity, mirth, joy, gaiety

Grass	submission, the fleeting quality of life, utility, usefulness
Grass, Lemon or Citronella	man's love, energizing, fresh start
Grevillea, *Banksia, Leucodendron, Protea*	steadfastness, diversity, loyalty, intent
Gypsophilia, *Baby's Breath*	pure heart, festivity, gaiety, everlasting love, innocence, happiness
Guelder Rose, *Snowball Viburnum*	winter, age, good news
Guernsey Lily, *Nerine Lily*	a nymph

H

Hand Flower Tree	warning
Hanging Amaranth, *Amaranth, Amaranthus caudatus, Love-lies-bleeding*	desertion, hopeless but not heartless, immortality
Hardenbergia, *Coral Pea, Happy Wanderer, Vine Lilac**	spirited, happiness, capability, ingenuity
Harebell, Common, *Campanula rotundifolia, Lady's Thimble*	submission, grief, humility
Hardy Geranium, *Crowsbill, Cranesbill*	constancy, availability, I desire to please, envy, wishes come true, imbecility, steadfast piety
Harlequin Flower, *Sparaxis*	one tear, the harlequin, tears of a clown
Hawkweed	quick-sighted
Hawthorne Tree	hope, love and marriage, banishes strife, protection
Hawthorne, foliage, flowers, wood	used in witchcraft, caution, hostility
Hazel Tree	reconciliation, peace, divination, marriage protection, poetic inspiration, meditation, knowledge, wisdom
Hazelnut	attraction, loss of inhibition, strengthens willpower, mystical powers, foresight
Heart's Ease, *Johnny-Jump-Up, Wild Pansy*	modesty, loving thoughts, you occupy my thoughts, think of me, happy thoughts, reflection, loyalty, merriment
Heath	solitude, independence, good fortune, good luck

Heath Myrtle, *Thryptomene, Calcynia, Grampians Heath Myrtle, Calynia, Kardomia, Baeckea imbricata and grandiflora**	sustenance, adversity, opulence, abundance
Heather	cleansing, good luck, admiration
Heather, white-color	good luck, protection, fulfillment of a dream, tranquility, wishes will come true
Heather, purple/lavender-color	beauty, worthy of admiration
Heavenly Bamboo, *Nandina*	my love will grow warmer
Hedysarum, *Sweetvetch*	agitation
Hedysarum gyrans, *Moving Plant*	agitation
Helenium, *Sneezeweed*	tears
Helesia Carolina, *Carolina Silverbell, Silverbell Tree**	surprise, epiphany, contentment, good fortune, prosperity, wonderment
Helianthemum, *Cistus, Rock Rose*	popular favor, security, safety
Helianthus, *Sunflower*	adoration, loyalty, you are splendid, best wishes, false riches, pride, my eyes only see you, haughtiness
Helichrysum italicum, *Everlasting, Immortelle*	never-ceasing memory, perpetual remembrance, endless love
Heliopsis, *False Sunflower, Oxeye Sunflower**	easy-going, subtleness, quiet, solitude, restful
Heliotrope	devotion, I adore you, herb of love, eternal love, faithfulness, intoxication, I love you, intoxicated with pleasure
Heliotrope, Cherry Pie	godly devotion, eagerness, forgiveness, acceptance
Heliotrope, Indian, *Turnsole*	intoxicated with joy, intoxication of love
Hellebore, *Christmas Rose, Lenten Rose*	relieve anxiety, protection against calumny, scandal, a beautiful year ahead, wit

Hellebore

Helmet Flower, *Aconite, Monkshood, Wolfsbane, Aconitum napellis, Turk's Cap, Friar's Cap*	misanthropy, treachery, poisonous words, symbol of crime, an enemy in disguise, chivalry, knight-errantry
Hemerocallis, *Day Lily*	wealth, success, pride, emblem of mother, coquetry, flirty
Hemerocallis, *Day Lily* (Chinese tradition)	emblem of the mother
Hemizygia, *Wild Sage, Candy Kisses**	cheerful, tenderness, sparkling personality, light-hearted, lively
Hemlock	you will cause my death, one of the four poisons, bad conduct
Hemp	fate, blessings of fate
Hemp, flowers*	achievement, reward, success, overcome diversity, stamina, perseverance
Henbane	for males to attract love from females, love spells, blemish, fault, imperfection
Hens and Chicks, *Aeonium, Echevaria, Houseleek, Sempervivum, Succulents*	long life, vivacity, domestic economy, welcome home, resilience, robust
Hepatica, *Liverwort, Anemone nobilis*	confidence, trust, apathy, your love makes me happy, constancy, permanence
Hesperis matronalis, *Dame's Rocket, Sweet Rocket, Queen's Rocket*	evening, evening star, danger, fashionable, you are the queen of coquettes!, rivalry
Heuchera, *Coral Bells*	challenge, hard work
Hibiscus, *Flower-of-an-Hour, Hibiscus trionum,* Bladder Hibiscus	delicate beauty, sweet or mild disposition
Hibiscus, Syriacus, common garden	gentle (Japanese tradition, Hanakotoba), delicate beauty, old royalty (Pacific Island tradition), immortality (Korean tradition) tropical love flower, consumed by love, celebration flower (Malaysian tradition)
Hibiscus, shrub	peace, happiness, rare beauty
Himalayan Blue Poppy, *Meconopsis, Blue Poppy*	mystery, attaining the impossible
Holly	domestic happiness, good will, protection, symbol of life, rebirth, enchantment, foresight
Holly Berries	Christmas joy, protection

Hollyhock (including Malva)	healing, forgiveness, ambition, fecundity, devotion to love, mother of family
Hollyhock, white-color	female ambition
Holly, Sea, *Eryngium*	attraction
Honesty, *Lunaria*, *Moonwort*, *Money Plant*	honesty, fascination, sincerity
Honey Bush, *Honey Flower*, *Melianthus*	sweet and secret love, speak low if you speak of love
Honeysuckle	generous and devoted affection, chains of love, I love you, sweetness of disposition, bond of love
Honeysuckle, coral color	the color of my fate, pursue your desire, experience pleasure, fidelity, generous and devoted love or affection, the bond of love
Honeysuckle, French	rustic beauty
Honeywort, *Blue Shrimp Plant*, *Cerinthe*, *Pride of Gibraltar******	tenacity, constancy, enduring, timeless affection
Hops	rest, sleep, mirth, beer
Hopseed Bush, *Dodonaea viscosa******	abundance in creativity, highly adaptable, impervious to adversity
Horehound	virtue, fire, health
Hornbeam	ornament
Horse Chestnut Tree	luxury, genius
Horsetail Rush, *Equisetum*	docility
Horseheal, *Elecampane*, *Elfdock*	tears
Hortensia, *Hydrangea*	devotion, remembrance, luck, success, happiness, mistrust, haven, protection, fickleness, you are cold, courageous woman, a boaster
Hosta	devotion
Houseleek, *Aeonium*, *Echeveria*, *Hens and Chicks*, *Sempervivum*, *Succulents*	long life, vivacity, domestic economy, welcome home, resilience, robust
Houstonia	content, innocence
Hoya, *Wax Plant*	sculptured loveliness, constancy, pure loveliness, susceptibility
Huckleberry	faith, simple pleasures

Hydrangea was long ago known as "boaster" because its blooms are large and showy but produce no seeds. Therefore, they are boastful.

Hyacinth	games, play, sport, constancy, flower of Apollo, gay flower, pure loveliness, joyful love, benevolence, love, jealousy
Hyacinth, blue-color	constancy, consistency, given to departing friends
Hyacinth, Grape	usefulness
Hyacinth, purple-color	consistency, loveliness, I'm sorry, please forgive me, sorrow
Hyacinth, apricot-, peach-, pink-, reds-colors	playful joy, play
Hyacinth, white-color	unobtrusive loveliness, I'll pray for you
Hyacinth, yellow-color	constancy, occasional jealousy
Hydrangea, *Hortensia*	devotion, remembrance, luck, success, happiness, mistrust, haven, protection, fickleness, you are cold, courageous woman, a boaster
Hydrangea, shrub	devotion to a noble cause or love, unveiling
Hydrangea, bright pink-color	feminine vitality
Hypericum, *St. John's Wort*	protection, animosity, superstition, you are a prophet, originality
Hyssop	cleansing, purification, holy herb that wards off evil and evil spirits

I

Iberis, *Candytuft*	sweetness, stoic beauty, indifference, wedding flower
Ice Plant, *Dew Plant*, *Ficoides*, *Fig Marigold*	serenade, old beau, rejected, cold-hearted, your looks freeze me, idleness, rejected addresses
Iceland Moss, *Cetraria*	health
Ilex paraguariensis, *Yerba Mate**	friendship, encouragement, cordiality, energy, mental clarity, upbeat happiness, communal happiness

Immortelle, *Everlasting, Helichrysum italicum*	never-ceasing memory, perpetual remembrance, endless love
Indian Cress, *Nasturtium*	resignation, victory, patriotism, jest, a warlike trophy
Indian Hawthorne*	versatility, honesty, industrious, energetic
Indian Hemp, *Dogsbane, Apocynum*	falsehood, I doubt you, deceit, figment
Indian Pink, *China Pink, Dianthus chinensis*	aversion
Indian Pink, double	always lovely
Indian Pink, single	you are aspiring
Indian Plum, *Osoberry*	privation
Indian Plantain, *Cacalia*	adulation, adoration
Ipomea purpurea, *Convolvulus major, Morning Glory*	extinquished hopes, affection, bonds of love, departure, greet the new day, busybody, coquetry
Iris, *Fleur-de-lis*	ardor, faith, eloquence, wisdom, promise in love, hope, valor, valued friendship, message, emblem of France, I burn with passion
Iris, European Wild Water	ardor, eloquence, promise, emblem of France, message
Iris, Dutch	message, my compliments, eloquence
Iris, Bearded	flame, passion of love
Iris, Sweet Flag	fitness
Iris, blue-color	faith, hope, wisdom, health
Iris, purple-color	wisdom, compliments
Iris, white-color	purity
Iris, yellow-color	passion
Iris, Wild, *Sweet Flag*	fitness and strength
Isatis tinctorial, *Asp of Jerusalem, Dyer's Woad, Woad*	modest merit
Itea virginica, *Sweetspire, Virginia Sweetspire**	you radiate kindness, dazzling personality
Ivy	constancy, wedded love, affection, reciprocal tenderness, fidelity in friendship, matrimony
Ivy Leaf	friendship
Ivy, sprig with tendrils	anxious to please, affection

Ivy Vine	matrimony, marriage
Ixia	happiness

J

Jack-in-the-Pulpit, *Arisaema*	continued happiness, love springs eternal
Jacob's Ladder, *Blue-flowered Greek Valerian*	rupture, split, come down, grace and elegance, wealth
Jacob's Rod, *Kingspear, Yellow Asphodel*	regret
Jade Plant/Tree, *Crassula ovata*	symbol of good fortune, wealth, health, happiness
Japanese Kerria, *Easter Rose, Kerria japonica, Pleniflora, Yellow Rose of Texas**	pleasant through the years, mature grace, perpetual beauty, be tough but stay beautiful, long beautiful
Japanese Medlar Plum, *Loquat*	pure and ardent love, personal warmth and comfort
Japanese Quince, *Chaenomeles*	symbolic of luck, prosperity, good fortune, love
Japanese Snowbell, *Styrax japonicus**	good fortune, health, encouragement, blessing
Japanese Wind Flower, *Anemone*	refusal, abandonment
Japanese Quince, *Chaenomeles japonica*	sincerity, symbol of love, luck, prosperity, good fortune, sincerity
Jasmine, flowering	amiability, transport of joy, I am so happy, wealth, grace, eloquence, candor
Jasmine, Azores	envy
Jasmine, Cape, *Gardenia*	ecstasy, feminine charm, transport of joy, I'm too happy, you're lovely, secret love, refinement
Jasmine, Carolina	separation, far country
Jasmine, Indian, *Sambac, Arabian Jasmine*	attraction, I attach myself to you, attachment, love, fidelity, devotion, dedication
Jasmine, Night-blooming, *Cestrum*	transient beauty
Jasmine, yellow-color	grace, elegance, modesty, first languor of love
Jasminum grandiflorum, *Spanish Jasmine*	sensuality, separation, I think you're sexy
Jerusalem Cross, *Maltese Cross, Lychnis, Campion, Catchfly*	snare, religious enthusiasm, sweetness, beauty, wit, sorrows, voyages, sun-beamed eyes, unchanging friendship, pretended love

Jerusalem Oak, *American Wormseed*	your love is reciprocated
Jockey's Cap, *Tiger Flower, Tigridia*	protection against cruelty, occasional cruelty, for once may pride befriend me!
Joe Pye Weed, *Eupatorium*	delay, love, respect
Jonquil	I desire a return of affection, desire, joys
Johnny-Jump-Up, *Heart's Ease, Wild Pansy*	modesty, loving thoughts, you occupy my thoughts, think of me, happy thoughts, reflection, loyalty, merriment
Joseph's Coat, *Alternanthera, Calico Plant*	favoritism
Judas Tree, *Cercis Tree, Redbud Tree*	love tree, unbelief, sometimes betrayal
Juncus, *Rush*	docility, navigation
Juniper	protection, welcome to new home, ingratitude
Justicia, *Brazilian Plume, Shrimp Plant*	perfection of female loveliness
Jute Mallow, *Corchorus*	impatient for happiness, absence, return quickly

K

Kalanchoe	popularity, endurance, lasting affection, I protect you, tolerant heart, a happy notice
Kalmia latifolia, *Calico Bush, Mountain Laurel*	ambition
Kangaroo Paws, *Anigozanthos manglesii*	unequal, oblique, distorted
Kardomia odontocalyx, *Calcynia, Calynia, Heath Myrtle, Thryptomene, Grampians Heath Myrtle, Baeckea imbricate and grandiflora**	sustenance, adversity, opulence, abundance
Kennedia, *Coral Vine*	mental beauty, intellectual beauty
Kerria japonica, *Easter Rose, Japanese Kerria, Pleniflora, Yellow Rose of Texas**	pleasant through the years, mature grace, perpetual beauty, be tough but stay beautiful, long beautiful
King-cups, *Trollis*	desire for riches
Kingspear, *Yellow Asphodel, Jacob's Rod*	regret

Kiwi Christmas Tree, *New Zealand Christmas Tree, Pohutukawa*	love, joy, marriage and bonds
Kniphofia, *Red Hot Poker, Torch Lily, Poker Plant**	caution, high-mindedness, disapproval
Knotweed, *Persicaria, Polygonum, Kiss-me-over-the-garden-gate, Prince's Feather*	vigilance, restoration
Koelreuteria, *Golden Rain Tree*	I claim your esteem, can mean dissention
Kumquat, branches with fruit	symbol of good fortune, wealth, health, happiness

L

Kumquat

Laburnum, *Golden Chain Tree*	forsaken, pensive beauty
Lady's Mantle, *Alchemilla mollis*	comforting love
Lady's Purse, *Calceolaria, Pocketbook Flower, Slipper Flower*	keep this for my sake
Lady's Seal, *Black Bryony*	be my support, stay
Lady's Slipper Orchid	capricious beauty, desirable, win and wear me
Lady's Smock, *Cuckoo Flower, Meadow Cress, Cardamine*	paternal error, ardor, paternal ardor, wit
Lady's Thimble, *Bellflower, Campanula rotundifolia, Common Harebell*	submission, grief, humility
Lady's-Tresses, *Spiranthes*	bewitching grace
Lagerstromia, *Crepe Myrtle*	eloquence
Lagunaria patersonia, *Primrose Tree*	inconstancy
Lamb's-ears, *Stachys byzantina*	softness, support, surprise
Lantana	rigor
Larch	audacity, boldness, can also mean fickleness
Larch Tree	protection, clear vision, wards off evil
Larkspur	levity, an open heart, lightness, ardent attachment, cheerfulness, fun
Larkspur, pink-color	fickleness
Larkspur, purple-color	haughtiness, big hearted, first love, ambition

Laurel, *Bay Tree*	glory, personal achievement, success, triumph, achievement in the arts, reward of merit
Laurel, common in flower	perfidy
Laurel, American, *California Bay Laurel, Oregon Myrtle*	falsehood, treachery
Laurel, Cherry	perfidy
Laurel, ground, *Trailing Arbutus, Mayflower*	welcome to a budding beauty, perseverance
Laurel leaf (single), *Bay Leaf (single)*	assured happiness, I change in death, strength
Laurel, Mountain, *Calico Bush, Kalmia latifolia*	ambition
Laurel, *Sweet Bay*	famous and notable, triumph of humanity
Laurestine, *Viburnum tinus*	a token, devoted to you, cheerful in adversity, delicate attentions
Laurustinus, *Viburnum tinus*	I die if I am neglected
Lavartera, *Tree Mallow*	sweet disposition
Lavender	devotion, luck, success, happiness, mistrust, healing, calming, soothing the passions of the heart, ardent attachment
Leatherleaf Fern	fascination, fidelity, I promise to be true, discretion
Leaves, dead	sadness, melancholy
Lemon and Limes	fidelity in love, zest, devine healing, removes sadness, brings affection
Lemon Balm	healing, fun, humor, love, relief, sharpens wit and understanding, pleasantry, sympathy
Lemon Blossom	everlasting and faithful love, fidelity, I promise to be true, discretion, prudence
Lemon leaves	fidelity in love, I promise to be true, brings love
Lemon Trees	zeal, fidelity, healing, love trees

Mistrust? Lavender? We don't think of mistrust when we think of lavender, but this meaning stems from the belief that since it is so affective at covering disagreeable odors, it should not be trusted, and therefore can represent mistrust.

Lemon Verbena	attracts love and fidelity, attracts opposite sex, unity
Lemongrass	energizing, fresh start, man's love
Leonotis leonurus, *Lion's Tail**	regal, creative, usefulness, elation, bliss
Lent Lily, *Naturalized Wild Daffodil*	sweet disposition
Lenten Rose, *Hellebores, Christmas Rose*	relieve my anxiety, protection against calumny, scandal, a beautiful year ahead, wit
Leopard Plant, *Ligularia, Bottle Rocket**	industrious, useful
Leptospermum, *Manuka, Tea Tree*	healing, strong health
Lettuce	cold-heartedness
Leucodendron, *Banksia, Grevillea, Protea*	steadfastness, diversity, loyalty, intent
Liatris, *Gay-Feather*	gaiety
Lichen	dejection, solitude, confidence
Licorice, wild	I declare against you
Ligularia, *Leopard Plant, Bottle Rocket**	industrious, useful
Lilac, *Syringa*	beauty, love, youth, earliest first love, fraternal love, memory, humility, pride, confidence, you shall be happy yet, do you still love me?
Lilac, purple-color	first emotions of love
Lilac, Vine, *Coral Pea, Happy Wanderer, Hardenbergia**	spirited, happiness, capability, ingenuity
Lilac, white-color	purity, youthful innocence, modest and pure emotions
Lilac, Wild, *Ceanothus**	reliability, rarity, constancy, vibrant personality
Lily	fruitfulness, purity, majesty, wealth, Chinese emblem for mother, honor, purity of heart, innocence, modesty
Lily, orange-color	I burn for you, flame, fascination, hatred or dislike
Lily, rose-color	rarity
Lily, scarlet-color	high souled aspirations, a lofty spirit
Lily, yellow-color	gaiety, happiness, I'm walking on air, gratitude, magnificent beauty, youthful innocence, golden prosperity, inquietude, falsehood

Lily, white-color	purity, majesty, modesty, virginity and sweetness, purity of spirit, sacred flower of virgin Mary, candor
Lily, Belladonna, *Amaryllis belladonna, Naked Ladies*	pure loveliness, I dream of you, you are a dream
Lily, Calla, *Arum Lily, Zantadeschia*	beauty and loveliness, maiden modesty, panache, magnificent beauty, overcome your challenges, rebirth and resurrection
Lily, Calla, lavender-color	femininity, refinement, grace and elegance, feminine beauty
Lily, Calla, yellow-color	joy, growth, change, lightheartedness, friendship
Lily, Calla, orange-color	energy, enthusiasm, success, confidence, passion for life
Lily, Calla, purple-color	royalty, accomplishment, admiration, dignity, tradition, success
Lily, Calla, white-color	purity and innocence
Lily, Canna	glorious, magnificent beauty
Lily, Cluster, *Brodiaea, Fool's Onion**	cultured, intellect, heartfelt, poetic, creative soul, inspired minds
Lily, Day, *Hemercalis*	wealth, pride, coquetry, emblem for mother
Lily, Day, *Homeroalis*	emblem of the mother
Lily, Eucharis, *Amazon Lily*	beauty, maidenly charms
Lily, Eucomis, *Pineapple Lily**	epiphany, prideful, majestic, abundance, deceptive charm
Lily, Imperial, *Crown Imperial, Fritillaria*	majesty, power, pride of birth, arrogance
Lily, Nerine, *Guernsey Lily*	a nymph
Lily, Palm, *Cordyline, Good Luck Plant, Hawaiian Ti Plant*	majesty, honor, purity of heart
Lily, Rain, *Zephyranthes*	expectation, fond caresses
Lily, Tiger	wealth and pride, majesty, honor, purity of heart
Lily, *Torch, Red Hot Poker, Poker Plant, Kniphofia**	caution, high-mindedness, disapproving
Lily, Viagra, *Dragon Arum, Dragonwort*	horror, dread, astonishment
Lily, Water	beauty, purity of heart, wisdom
Lily, Winter, *Clivia, Clive**	you enhance my life, an ornament of beauty and distinction

Lily of the Nile, *Agapanthus*	love letters, love, enduring spiritual beauty and purity
Lily of the Valley	return of happiness, sweetness, tears of the Virgin Mary, you've made my life complete, delicacy
Lily of the Valley (Irish tradition)	fairy ladders, the ladder to heaven
Lily of the Valley, plants	protects a garden against evil, evil spirits
Lily of the Valley shrub, *Pieris, Andromeda*	happy thoughts, happiness through the ages, self-sacrifice
Lime, tree and flowers	conjugal love, wedded love, matrimony, fornication
Limonium, *Statice, Sea Lavender*	never ceasing remembrance, sympathy, lasting beauty, dauntlessness
Linden, American	marital virtues, conjugal love, matrimony, conjugal fidelity
Lint, White Oak	I feel my obligation
Lion's Tail, *Leonotis leonurus**	regal, creative, usefulness, elation, bliss
Lisianthus	showy, kind thoughts, outgoing
Living Plants	growth, everlasting
Live Oak	liberty, manliness
Liverwort, *Anemone nobilis, Hepatica*	your love makes me happy, constancy, permanence, confidence, trust, apathy
Lobelia, spiking	distinguished
Lobelia, low-growing	malevolence
Lobelia, Cardinal	distinction
Locust	affection beyond the grave, platonic love
London-Pride, *Saxifraga*	frivolity, fun, gaiety, lightheartedness
Loosestrife, *Lysimachia*	wishes granted
Loosestrife, Purple, *Lythrum salicaria*	pretension
Loquat, *Japanese Medlar Plum*	pure and ardent love, personal warmth and comfort
Lords and Ladies, *Arum, Arum Lily, Cuckoopint*	ardor, zeal, ferocity, deceit
Loropetalum, *Chinese Fringe Flower**	fun and flirty, wit, merriment, joy

Lotus	purity, chastity, elegance, holy spiritual flower, recantation, forgetful of the pat, eloquence, a love match, silence
Lotus, plant	estranged love
Lote Tree	concord
Lovage	strength
Love-in-a-Puff vine, *Balloon Plant**	surprise, charming, sultry, heart, my heart, delicate love
Love-in-a-mist, *Nigella*	you puzzle me, perplexity, bewilderment, independence, prosperity
Love-lies-bleeding, *Amaranth, Amaranthus caudatus, Hanging Amaranth*	desertion, hopeless but not heartless, immortality, recantation
Lunaria, *Honesty, Moonwort, Money Plant*	honesty, fascination, sincerity
Lucerne, *Alfalfa*	life
Lungwort, *Pulmonaria*	thou art my life
Lupine	voraciousness, imagination, dejection
Lychee, *Lichee*	summer, a wish for children, marriage celebration
Lychnis, Campion, Jerusalem Cross, Maltese Cross, Catchfly	snare, religious enthusiasm, sweetness, beauty, wit, sorrows, voyages, sun-beam'd eyes, unchanging friendship, pretended love
Lychnis Flos-Cuculi, *Meadow Lychnis, Ragged Robin*	wit, sweetness, beauty, ardor
Lysmachia, *Creeping Jenny*	forgiveness, womb plant
Lysmachia, *Loosestrife*	wishes granted
Lythrum salicaria, *Purple Loosestrife*	pretension

M

Madder	calumny, or can as a protectant against slander, character assassination
Madder, yellow-color	tranquility
Madrone, *Arbutus, Madrona, Strawberry Tree*	thee only do I love, you are my only love, esteem and love

Magic Flower, *Cupid's Bower,* *Achimenes*	such worth is rare
Magnolia (Chinese tradition)	love of nature
Magnolia, deciduous	bonds of love, secret bond of love
Magnolia, Grandiflora, *Laurel-leaf Magnolia*	proud and peerless, dignity, splendid beauty, purity, feminine, nobility
Magnolia, Saucer, *Tulip Tree*	bonds of love, fame
Magnolia, Swamp	perseverance
Maidenhair Fern	discretion, secret bond of love
Maidenhair Tree, *Ginkgo biloba**	longevity, solitary beauty, enlightenment, profound endurance
Maize, *Corn*	riches, gift of mother earth
Mallow	good and kind, mildness, delicate beauty, sweetness, consumed by love
Mallow, Syrian	consumed by love
Mallow, Wax, *Achania malvaviscus,* *Turk's Cap Mallow*	reserve
Maltese Cross, *Jerusalem Cross,* *Lychnis, Campion, Catchfly*	snare, religious enthusiasm, sweetness, beauty, wit, sorrows, voyages, sun-beam'd eyes, unchanging friendship, pretended love
Manchineel	falsehood, I wound to sooth, betrayal
Mandevilla, *Chilean Jasmine,* *Dipladenia, Rocktrumpet**	attraction, delicate beauty, gentility, delectable, sensitive, susceptible, sometimes wreckless or thoughtless
Mandrake	horror, rarity, or extraordinary
Manuka, *Leptospermum, Tea Tree*	healing, strong health
Maple	elegance, reserve, love, retirement, draws together
Maple Tree	success, abundance
Maple, Japanese	baby's hands
Marguerite Daisy	variety, oracle of the meadows
Marigold	health, sacred golden light, flower of Mary: "Mary's gold," overcomes grief, despair, jealousy, pretty love
Marigold, African	vulgar minds
Marigold and Cypress (pairing)	despair

Magnolia

Marigold, Cape, *African Daisy, Dimorphotheca*	foreknowledge
Marigold, Fig, *Dew Plant, Ficoides, Ice Plant*	serenade, old beau, rejected, cold-hearted, your looks freeze me, idleness, rejected addresses
Marigold, French	comforts the heart, jealousy, overcomes jealousy
Marigold, Pot, *Calendula*	health, joy, remembrance, constancy, the sun, affection, disquietude, grief, jealousy, misery, cares, constancy, presage, overcomes trouble
Marigold, Prophetic (as used in pillows)	prediction
Marjoram, Hop, *Dittany of Crete*	birth, childbirth
Marjoram, Sweet, *Oregano*	consolation, happiness, joy, kindness, illusion or delusion, blushes
Marsh Mallow, *Althea officianalis*	beneficence, to cure, persuasion, consumed by love, charity, humanity
Marvel of Peru	timidity, flee, dread love
Mask flower, *Alonsoa*	gratitude
Masterwort, *Astrantia*	strength, power, courage, protection
Mayday Flower, *Anemone pulsatilla, Pasque Flower, Wind Anemone*	you have no claims, unpretentious
Mayflower, *Ground Laurel, Trailing Arbutus*	welcome to a budding beauty, perseverance
Meadow Cress, *Cardamine, Cuckoo Flower, Lady's Smock*	paternal error, ardor, parental ardor, wit
Meadow Lychnis, *Lychnis Flos-Cuculi, Ragged Robin*	wit, sweetness, beauty, ardor
Meadow Rue, *Thalictrum*	divination
Meadow Saffron, *Colchicum*	my best days are past
Meadowsweet	uselessness
Meconopsis, *Himalayan Blue Poppy, Blue Poppy*	mystery, attaining the impossible
Melia azedarach, *Chinaberry, Persian Lilac, Pride of India*	dissension, rebellion
Melianthus, *Honey Bush, Honey Flower*	sweet and secret love, speak low if you speak of love
Mercury, *Dog's Mercury, Mercurialis*	goodness

Mexican Firebrush, *Belvedere, Mock Cypress*	I declare against you
Mezereum, *February Daphne*	desire to please, a flirt
Michaelmas Daisy, *New England Aster, Belgian Aster*	afterthought, memories, farewell, healthy emotions, autumn, love and contentment, variety, delicacy, love vibrations
Mignonette, *Resida*	your qualities surpass your charms, health, worth, happiness of the moment
Milfoil	war
Milkvetch, *Astragulus*	your presence softens my pain
Milkweed, *Asclepias, Butterfly Weed, Swallow-wort*	hope in misery, medicine, cure for heartache, let me go
Milkwort	hermitage, solitude, desolate
Mimosa, *Sensitive Plant*, includes Mimosa Tree, Persian Silk Tree	sensibility, delicate feelings, prudery, secret, chastity, bashful modesty, secret love, fastidious, exquisite
Mint	warmth of feeling, virtue, protection from illness, let us be friends again, you are virtuous
Mint, Lemon	cheerfulness, hominess, virtue
Mistletoe	I surmount all difficulties, I want to be kissed, kiss me, affection, obstacles to be overcome
Mock Cypress, *Belvedere, Mexican Firebrush*	I declare against you
Mock Orange, *Philadelphus*	brotherly love, counterfeit, memories, resourcefulness, alternatives
Molucca Bean, *Nickernut*	good-luck charm
Monarda, *Bee Balm, Bergamot*	compassion, sweet virtues, your wiles are irresistible!
Monkshood, *Aconite, Anconitum napellis, Helmet Flower, Wolfsbane Turk's Cap, Friar's Cap*	misanthropy, treachery, poisonous words, symbol of crime, an enemy in disguise, chivalry, knight-errantry
Moonflower, vining	I only dream of love, night, instability
Moonwort, *Honesty, Lunaria, Money Plant*	honesty, fascination, sincerity
Morning Glory, *Ipomaea purpurea, Convolvulus major*	extinquished hopes, affection, bonds of love, departure, greet the new day, busybody, coquetry

Morning Glory, Dwarf, *Convolvulus minor, Tricolor Bindweed*	repose, night, obstinacy, humility
Morning Glory, red-color	I am attached to you, attachment
Moschatel (Hollowroot/ Adoxa, Five-faced Bishop, Hollowroot, Muskroot)	weakness
Mourning Bride Scabiosa, *Scabiosa autopurpruea, Black Mourning Bride*	I have lost all, unfortunate attachment
Moss	maternal love, charity
Moss, Flowering, *Pyxie*	life is sweet
Moss, *Hairmoss, Fat Choy*	secret
Moss Rose, *Portulaca*	superior, confession of love
Mossy Saxifrage, *Rockfoils*	affection
Moth Orchid, *Phalaenopsis Orchid*	evening joy, you are a belle, you flatter me
Motherwort	secret love, concealed love
Mountain Ash, *Rowan, Mountainash Tree, Witchwood Tree*	ambition, healing, empowerment, divination, tree of life, treachery, prudence, protection, with me you are safe, purification
Mountain Laurel, *Calico Bush* (Kalmia latifolia)	ambition
Mouse-ear Chickweed, *Cerasium*	simplicity
Moving Plant, *Hedysarum gyrans*	agitation
Mugwort, *Artemisia vulgaris,*	dignity, tranquility, peace, happiness
Mulberry, black, tree or fruit	devotedness, I shall not survive you, sadness
Mulberry, white, tree or fruit	wisdom, prudence
Mullein, Common, *Verbascum*	good nature, take courage, health
Mushroom (any kind)	suspicion, surprise, rapid fortune

*The mulberry is esteemed as the wisest of all trees because it never expands its buds until all danger of frost has past. Hence, its meaning—*wisdom*.*

Musk Monkeyflower, *Eyebright, Musk-Plant*	be bolder, weakness
Mustard Plant, *Senvy*	smart, indifference
Myrobalan Plum, *Cherry Plum*	privation
Myroxylon, *Balsam of Peru*	cure, cure for heartache
Myrrh, *Sweet Cicely, Chervil*	sincerity, gladness
Myrtle	fidelity, love, marriage, married bliss, passion, Hebrew emblem of marriage, love in absence, remembrance, love positive
Myrtle, Heath, *Kardomia odontocalyx, Baeckea imbricate and grandiflora, Calcynia, Calynia, Grampians Heath Myrtle, Thryptomene**	sustenance, adversity, opulence, abundance
Myrtle, Oregon, *American Laurel, California Bay Laurel*	falsehood, treachery
Myrtle, Wax, *Bayberry*	good luck, instruction, discipline, duty

N

Naked Ladies, *Amaryllis belladonna, Belladonna Lily*	pure loveliness, I dream of you, you are a dream
Nandina, *Heavenly Bamboo*	my love will grow warmer
Narcissus, *Daffodil (common)*	regard, respect, unrequited love, sunshine, the sun shines when I am with you, chivalry, you're the only one
Narcissus, *Paperwhite*	self-esteem, hope, prosperity, renewal, gracefulness, respect, self-love, national flower of Wales, aphrodisiac, sweetness, you are sweet
Narcissus, double	female ambition
Nasturtium, *Indian Cress*	patriotism, jest, a warlike trophy, resignation, victory
Nasturtium, pastel shades	maternal love, charity
Nemophila menziesii, *Baby Blue Eyes*	success, prosperity, safety, security, open-heartedness
Nepeta mussinii, *Catmint**	mischievous, good-natured, spirited, whimsical, I want to have fun!
Nerine, Lily, *Guernsey Lily*	a nymph

Nerium, *Oleander, Rosebay*	caution, beware, mistrust
Nettles, *Urtica dioica*	slander, you are spiteful, you are cruel, don't sting me
New Zealand or Kiwi Christmas Tree, *Pohutukawa*	love, joy, marriage and bonds
Nickernut, *Molucca Bean*	good-luck charm
Nigella, *Love-in-a-Mist*	you puzzle me, perplexity, bewilderment, independence, prosperity
Night-blooming Cereus, *Night Bloom Cactus*	transient beauty, radiant, sweet beauty, modest genius, a spectacular moment
Nightshade, *Bittersweet*	falsehood, silence, dark thoughts, bitter truth, sorcery, spell, witchcraft, skepticism, truth, a platonic love
Nuts	stupidity

O

Oak	hospitality, independence, strength, bravery, majesty, wisdom, protection, potency and fertility, endurance, healing, strength and money, love of country
Oak Leaves	bravery, strength, humanity
Oak, Live	liberty, manliness
Oak, White	independence
Oats	music, I love your music, you satisfy me
Obedient Plant, *Physostegia*	obedience
Oenothera, *Evening Primrose, Sun Cups, Sun Drops*	happiness, happy love, sometimes inconstancy, mildness
Oleander, *Nerium, Rosebay*	caution, beware, distrust
Olives	peace and prosperity
Olive Tree	peace, fruitfulness, security and money
Olive Branch	peace, happiness in love
Olive, Russian	bitterness
Olive, Sweet or Tea, *Osmanthus*	protection, happiness, good fortune, prosperity, dreams, reward of literary merit
Onionweed	regret
Ononis, *Restharrow*	obstacle

Ophrys, *Black Spider Orchid*	dexterity
Opuntia, *Prickly Pear*	I burn
Orange Tree	generosity, sweetness
Orange Blossom	bridal festivities, your purity equals your loveliness, brings wisdom, chastity, eternal love, purity, generosity, magnificence
Orange-color flowers (any type)	chastity
Orange, fruit	symbolic of golden pieces, good luck, fortune
Orchid	love, luxury, nobility, refinement, a belle, rare beauty, Chinese symbol for many children, thoughtfulness, you flatter me
Orchid (Asian traditions)	symbols of strength, endurance, good energy, luck
Orchid, Bee	Industry, occasional mistake
Orchid, Black Spider, *Ophrys*	dexterity
Orchid, Butterfly	gaiety
Orchid, Cattleya	matronly grace, mature charms
Orchid, Cymbidium	beauty, love, luxury, magnificence, long life
Orchid, Dendrobium	a belle, beautiful lady, precious treasure
Orchid, Lady's Slipper	capricious beauty, desirable, win and wear me
Orchid, Oncidium	a beautiful lady or person, a belle
Orchid, Phalaenopsis, *Moth Orchid*	evening joy, you are a belle, you flatter me
Orchis, Bee, *Early Purple Orchid*	error, industry, beauty
Oregano, *Sweet Marjoram*	consolation, happiness, joy, kindness, illusion or delusion, blushes
Osmanthus, *Sweet Olive, Tea Olive*	protection, happiness, good fortune, prosperity, dreams, reward of literary merit
Osmunda, *Royal and Cinnamon Fern*	I dream of thee, reverie
Osoberry, *Indian Plum*	privation
Oxalis, *acetosella, trifolium repens, Four-Leaf Clover*	faith, hope, luck, love; when given to another: luck be with you, be mine; when given to a lover: you belong to each other

Cattleya Orchid

Oxalis, *Shamrock, including trifolium dubium*	Ireland, lightheartedness, luck, loyalty, wit
Oxeye Daisy	patience, be patient, attracts wealth, obstacle, token of affection
Oxeye Sunflower, *Heliopsis, False Sunflower**	easygoing, subtleness, quiet, solitude, restful

P

Palm	victory, dignity, success
Palm, Coconut	tropical tree of life and abundance
Pandanus	magic, devotion, death and bad luck
Pansy, Wild, *Heart's Ease, Johnny-Jump-Up*	modesty, loving thoughts, you occupy my thoughts, think of me, happy thoughts, reflection, loyalty, merriment
Paperwhite Narcissus	self-esteem, hope, prosperity, renewal, gracefulness, respect, self-love, national flower of Wales, aphrodisiac, sweetness
Parsley	festivity, gratitude, thanks, useful knowledge, a feast
Parrot's Bill, *Clianthus*	self seeking, worldliness
Pasque Flower, *Anemone pulsatilla, Mayday Flower, Wind Anemone*	you have no claims, unpretentious
Passion Flower	Christian faith, belief, Holy love, religious passion, faith, violent pain of love, susceptibility
Patience Dock	Patience
Paulownia, *Princess Tree*	benevolence
Peacock Orchid, *Gladiolus acidanthera*	distinction
Pea, general	appoint a meeting, lasting pleasure (everlasting)
Pea, flower	mental beauty
Pea, Sweet	delicate pleasures, departure, tender memory, good-bye, blissful pleasure, thank you for a lovely time
Peach	feminine softness, longevity, your qualities, like your charms, are unequaled
Peach, flowering	I am your captive, love, divination, longevity, long life, constancy

Pear	affection, health, hope, longevity
Pear, blossom	affections, lasting friendship, more than just lovely
Pear Tree	comfort
Pelargoniums, *Geraniums (general)*	comfort, conjugal affection, true friend, peaceful mind
Pelargonium sidoides	recall, admiration
Pennyroyal	flee away!
Penstemon, *Beardtongue*	spiritual knowledge, understanding
Peony	hands full of cash, welcome, compassion, happy marriage and happy life, aphrodisiac, hardiness, bashful shame, anger, a frown, heaviness
Pepper, flower	satirical thoughts
Peppermint	warmth of feeling, cordiality
Peppermint Willow, *Agonis, Burgundy Willow, Willow Myrtle**	grace, poise, versatility, attraction, balance
Periwinkle, blue-color	early friendship, sweet memories, lifelong friendship, tender recollections
Periwinkle, white-color	pleasing reminiscences
Perovskia, *Russian Sage*	knowledge and wisdom
Persea borbonia, *Redbay, Scrubbay, Swampby, Tisswood*	memory
Persian Lilac, *Chinaberry, Melia azedarach, Pride of India*	dissension, rebellion
Persian Silk Tree, *Mimosa Tree, also includes Sensitive Plan, Mimosa*	sensibility, delicate feelings, prudery, secret, chastity, bashful modesty, secret love, fastidious, exquisite
Persicaria, *Knotweed, Polygonum,* Kiss-me-over-the-garden-gate, Prince's Feather	vigilance, restoration
Persimmon	resistance, bury me amid nature's beauty
Persimmon, blossom	I shall surprise you by and by, bury me amid nature's beauty
Peruvian Heliotrope	devotion
Peruvian Lily, *Alstromeria*	friendship, devotion, aspiring, wealth, prosperity, fortune, strength
Petunia	resentment, anger, your presence soothes me

Pheasant's Eye, *Adonis*	sorrowful remembrance, painful recollections
Philadelphus, *Mock Orange*	brotherly love, counterfeit, memories, resourcefulness, alternatives
Philomis, *Jerusalem Sage*	earthly delights, pride of ownership
Philotheca, *Eriostemon**	my beloved, dear to me, loved
Phlox	proposal of love, sweet dreams, unanimity, our souls united
Phlox, star-shaped	affability, trying to please you, sweet dreams
Physostegia, *Obedient Plant*	obedience
Pieris, *Lily of the Valley shrub, Andromeda*	happy thoughts, happiness through the ages, self-sacrifice
Pigeon Berry	indifference
Pimpernel, *Anagallis*	change, fickleness
Pimpernel, scarlet	appointment, assignation, change
Pincushion, *Scabiosa*	admiration, widowhood, comfort in loss of someone
Pine	endurance, loyalty, vigorous life, hardiness, light, boldness
Pine, boughs, foliage	hope, philosophy, purification, friendship occasionally pity
Pinecone	conviviality, renewal of life
Pine, Pitch	philosophy, time and faith
Pine, Spruce	hope in adversity
Pine Tree	purification of health, fortune, fertility, posterity, daring, spiritual energy, vigorous life
Pineapple	you are perfect, perfection, luck
Pineapple Lily, *Eucomis**	epiphany, prideful, majestic, abundance, but can also mean deceptive charm
Pineapple Sage	esteem, hospitality, happy home
Pink, *Dianthus barbatus, Sweet William*	love, affection, boldness, pure affection, classic love flower, childhood, memory, grant me one smile, perfection, finesse
Pink, China, *Dianthus chinensis, Indian Pink*	aversion
Pink, Indian double	always lovely
Pink, Indian single	you are aspiring, always lovely

Pink, Mountain	aspiring
Pink, Garden	childishness
Pink, double, red-color	pure and ardent love
Pink, single	pure love
Pink, variegated	always lovely and happy, refusal with greatest respect
Pink, white-color	ingeniousness, talent
Pink, yellow-color	unreasonableness, a difficult love
Pittosporum, *Cheesewood**	deviate from difficulties, conquer, shelter, to bring certainty, comfort, blessings
Plane Tree	genius, umbrage
Plantain	pilgrimage, well-trodden path, independence, strength of faith
Plantain, Indian, *Cacalia*	adulation, adoration
Platycodon, *Balloon Flower*	return of a friend is desired
Pleniflora, *Easter Rose, Japanese Kerria, Kerria japonica, Yellow Rose of Texas*	pleasant through the years, mature grace, perpetual beauty, be tough but stay beautiful, long beautiful
Pleurisy Root	heartache cure
Plum	promise, hope, keep your promise
Plum, Cherry, *Myrobalan Plum*	privation
Plum Tree	fidelity, longevity
Plum, Indian	deprivation, want and need, austerity
Plum, wild	independence
Plum, fruit	courage, happiness, perseverance
Plum, blossom	be of good cheer, keep your promises, fidelity
Plumbago	holy wishes, antidote
Plumeria	Shelter, Protection
Pocketbook Flower, *Calceolaria, Lady's Purse, Slipper Flower*	keep this for my sake
Pohutukawa, *New Zealand or Kiwi Christmas Tree*	love, joy, marriage and bonds
Poinsettia	be of good cheer
Poker Plant, *Red Hot Poker, Torch Lily, Kniphofia**	caution, high-mindedness, disapproving

Polyanthus, *(a Primrose with clusters of flowers on one stem)*	pride of riches, confidence, elegance, the heart's mystery, someone seeks to seduce you, unpatronized merit
Polyanthus, crimson-color	inconstancy
Polyanthus, lilac-color	confidence
Polygala, *Sweet Pea Shrub*	hermitage
Polygonatum, *Solomon's Seal*	secret
Polygonum, *Knotweed, Persicaria, Kiss-me-over-the-garden-gate, Prince's Feather*	vigilance, restoration
Pomegranate	good luck, elegance, occasionally foolishness, royalty, perfect friendship, fatuity
Pomegranate, flower	mature elegance
Pomegranate, fruit	union, elegance
Poor Man's Asparagus, *Bonus-henricus, Good-King-Henry*	benevolence, goodness
Poplar	endure and conquer, courage, time
Poplar, black	courage
Poplar, Tulip	fame, retirement, rural happiness, among the noblest
Poplar, white-color	time, youth
Poppy	eternal sleep, oblivion, imagination, pleasure, wealth, consolation, repose, consolation to the sick
Poppy, black-color	rebirth, rejuvenation, farewell, death
Poppy, blue color, *Himalayan Blue Poppy, Meconopsis*	mystery, attaining the impossible
Poppy, California, *Eschscholtzia*	sweetness
Poppy, corn	ephemeral charms
Poppy, red-color	wealth, success, true love, pleasure, fantastic extravagance
Poppy, variegated	flirtation, dreaminess
Poppy, white-color	consolation, rest, eternal sleep, peace, dormant affection, eternal love, virtue, purity, reverence, innocence, humility, my bane, my antidote
Poppy, yellow-color	wealth, success
Poppy Mallow	wine cups

Portulaca, *Moss Rose*	superior, confessions of love
Potato	benevolence
Potato Vine, *Solanum, Purple Robe Bush*	loneliness, smile, true
Potentilla, *Cinquefoil*	maternal affection, beloved daughter, beloved child
Porcelain Vine, *Ampelopsis quinquefolia, also includes Virginia Creeper, Woodbine*	I cling to you both in sunshine and shade, fraternal love, shyness
Prickly Pear, *Opuntia*	I burn
Pride of India, *Chinaberry, Melia azedarach, Persian Lilac*	dissension, rebellion
Pride of Gibraltar, *Blue Shrimp Plant, Cerinthe, Honeywort**	tenacity, constancy, enduring, timeless affection
Primrose, *Primula, vulgaris-type (single flowers on one stem)*	early youth, I can't live without you, young love, happiness, satisfaction, believe me, trust in me, the first, prime
Primrose, *Primula vulgaris,* bright colors	warmth and merit
Primrose, *Primula vulgaris,* pink shades	womanly love, womanhood
Primrose, *Primula vulgaris,* red-color	unpatronized or neglected merit, early youth, sadness
Primrose, *Primula vulgaris,* white-color	womanhood, also womanly love
Primrose, Evening, *Sun Cups, Sun Drops, Oenothera*	happiness, happy love, mildness
Primrose Tree, *Lagunaria patersonia*	inconstancy
Primula auricula, *Auricula*	painting, pride of newly acquired fortune, wealth is not always happiness
Prince's Feather, *Amaranth*	warmth and caring, I blush for you, unfading love
Prince's Feather, *Persicaria, Polygonum, Knotweed, Kiss-me-over-the-garden-gate*	vigilance, restoration
Princess Flower, *Glory Flower, Tibouchina urvilleana*	glorious beauty, glory, protection against cruelty, occasionally cruelty, for once may pride befriend me!
Princess Tree, *Paulownia*	benevolence

Privet	mildness, prohibitive
Protea, *Banksia, Grevillea, Leucodendron*	steadfastness, diversity, loyalty, intent
Pulmonaria, *Lungwort*	thou art my life
Pumpkin	grossness, coarseness
Purple Clover	provident
Purple Robe Bush, *Potato Vine, Solanum*	loneliness, smile, true
Pussy-willow	never-ceasing remembrance, motherhood, recovery from illness
Pussy-willow (Asian traditions)	symbol of luck, prosperity, good fortune, love
Pyrus Japonica	fairies' fire
Pyxie, *Flowering Moss*	life is sweet

Q

Quaker Ladies, *Bluets*	contentment
Quaking Grass	agitation, my thoughts are uneasy, frivolity
Quamoclit, *Cypress Vine*	busybody, curiosity
Queen Anne's Lace, *Ammi majus, Bishop's Flower*	haven, sanctuary, protection, warmth, fantasy
Queen of the Prairie, *Filipendula rubra*	farsighted outlook
Queen's Rocket, *Sweet Rocket, Dame's Rocket,* Hesperis matronalis	fashionable, you are the queen of coquettes!, evening, evening star, danger, rivalry
Quince	cheers my soul, temptation, represents a choice, abundance
Quince, flower	symbol of love, sincerity
Quince, *Japanese Quince, aponica, Chaenomeles*	sincerity, symbol of love, luck, prosperity, good fortune

Quince

R

Ragged Robin, *Lychnis Flos-Cuculi*, *Meadow Lychnis*	wit, sweetness, beauty, ardor
Ragweed, *Ambrosia*	love returned, will you return my love?
Ragwort, *Senecio*	I am humble but proud
Rain Lily, *Zephyranthes*	expectation, fond caresses
Ranunculus	attraction, charming, you are rich in attractions, I am dazzled by your charms, pride
Ranunculus, wild	ingratitude
Raspberry	gentle-heartedness, remorse
Ray Grass	vice
Red Catchfly, *Silene*	youthful love
Red Hot Poker, *Torch Lily, Poker Plant, Kniphofia**	caution, high-mindedness, disapproving
Redbay, *Persea borbonia, Scrubbay, Swampby, Tisswood*	memory
Redbud Tree, *Cercis Tree, Judas Tree*	love tree, unbelief, sometimes betrayal
Redosier, Dogwood, *Red-osier Dogwood*	frankness
Redwood*	robust, durability, ingenious, resourceful, timeless, eternal love
Reed	complaisance, music, symbol of music
Reed, feathery	indiscretion
Reed, flowering	confidence in heaven
Reed, split	indiscretion
Resida, *Mignonette*	your qualities surpass your charms, health, worth, happiness of the moment
Restharrow, *Ononis*	obstacle
Rhododendron	danger, beware, planted to ward off danger
Rhubarb	advice
Ribes aureum, *Blackcurrant**	happy, ethereal, elation, humor, bliss
Ribes, *Currant*	thy frown will kill me

Rice Flower*	longevity, richness, abundance, I am happy with you, you are my lifeblood, brilliant
Rock Rose, *Cistus, Helianthemum*	popular favor, security, safety
Rocket, Dame's, *Hesperis matronalis, Dame's Violet, Sweet Rocket*	evening, evening star, danger, rivalry, queen of coquettes
Rockfoils, *Mossy Saxifrage*	affection
Rocktrumpet, *Chilean Jasmine, Dipladenia, Mandevilla**	attraction, delicate beauty, gentility, delectable, sensitive, susceptible
Rose	beauty, congratulations, friendship, love, classic love flower, reward of virtue, ephemeral beauty
Rose, Austrian	you are all that is lovely
Rose, black-color	farewell, symbol of death
Rose, Bridal	happiness, happy love
Rose, brown-color	fascination, anticipation
Rose, burgundy-color	unconscious beauty, beauty within
Rose, Cabbage	ambassador of love
Rose Campion, *Silene coronaria, Lychnis coronaria*	only deserve my love
Rose, Carolina	love is dangerous
Rose, Centifolia/Hundred-leafed	graces, the finest, pride
Rose, China	beauty always new
Rose, champagne-color	devotion, vitality
Rose, cherry-red-color	merriment, sweetness of character
Rose, Cinnamon	precocity, without pretention
Rose, coral-color	good fortune, longevity, desire
Rose, cream-color	perfection, richness, charming, thoughtful, gracious
Rose, Damask	freshness, Persian Ambassador of Love, beauty ever new, young and brilliant, brilliant complexion
Rose, daily (given to another daily)	I aspire to your smile
Rose, dark crimson-color	mourning
Rose, deep pink-color	thankfulness, gratitude

Rose

Rose, deep red-color	love, admiration, embarrassment, bashful, shame
Rose, Dog	pleasure and pain
Rose, faded	alas for fleeting beauty, beauty is fleeting
Rose, full-bloom	beauty at its finest, beauty at its fullest, you are beautiful
Rose, full-blown over two buds	secrecy
Rose, Général Jacqueminot	I am true
Rose, gilded	excess
Rose, golden-color	absolute achievement
Rose, green-color	freshness, health, liberty, I am from Mars, we are worlds apart
Rose, Guelder, *Snowball Viburnum*	winter, age, good news
Rose, half-blown	timid love
Rose, hundred-leaved	graces, pride
Rose, Japanese Pleniflora, *Easter Rose, Japanese Kerria, Kerria japonica, Pleniflora, Yellow Rose of Texas**	pleasant through the years, mature grace, perpetual beauty, be tough but stay beautiful, long beautiful
Rose, lavender-color	dignity, rarity, enchantment, love at first sight, grace, elegance, sweet thoughts, majesty, refinement, opulence, enchantment
Rose, leaves or leaf	you may hope, I will never bed
Rose, Maiden Blush	if you love me, you will find it out
Rose, Maréchal Niel	yours, heart and soul
Rose, monthly (given to another monthly)	beauty always new
Rose, Moss, *Portulaca*	superior, confession of love
Rose, Multiflora	grace
Rose, Mundi	variety
Rose, Musk	capricious beauty, charming
Rose, Musk, cluster	charming
Rose, orange-color	fascination, desire, speak your desire, secret love
Rose, peach, soft pink-color	admiration, immortality, modesty, sociability, friendship, grace, joy
Rose, peach-color	appreciation, gratitude, you are tender and loving

Rose, hybrid perpetual	unfading love
Rose, pink-color	perfect happiness, secret love, sweetness, indecision, admiration, perfect love, grace, beauty, believe me, thank you
Rose, pink (soft and light shades)	desire, passion, love of life, youth energy, joy, grace, I understand, sympathy, I am sorry, especially when ill
Rose, pink- and white-color	I love you still and always
Rose, Pompon	prettiness, genteel
Rose, Porcelana	admiration
Rose, purple-color	sorrow
Rose, red-color	beauty, charm, desire, I love you, joy, passion, desire, romance, passionate love, true love and beauty, unity, romantic love
Rose, red- and white-color	creative force, joy, unity, sufferings of love, fires of the heart
Rose, red-withered	ended love, our love is over
Rose, *rubiginosa, Eglantine, Sweet Briar, European*	poetry, a poetic person, I wound to heal
Rose, Sterling Silver	love at first sight
Rose, striped	warmth of heart, summer
Rose, rose-colored	beauty, love, pride, shyness
Rose, single (not red)	simplicity
Rose, single (red)	new love, I love you, I still love you, simplicity, beauty
Rose, single full bloom	I love you, I still love you, engagement
Rose, *Sweet Briar, American*	simplicity
Rose, *Sweet Briar, European, Rosa rubiginosa, Eglantine*	I wound to heal, poetry, a poetic person
Rose, Sweet Briar, yellow-color	decrease in love, let us forget it
Rose, Sweetheart and Minis	sweetheart, darling, dear one, my honey
Rose, Tea	I'll remember always, I will always remember you
Rose, thornless	early attachment, gratitude, love at first sight, sincere friend, occasional ingratitude
Rose, thorn	danger
Rose, thorny	pleasure and pain

Roses, two in full bloom	secrecy
Rose, white-color	beauty, love, respect, silence, unity, I am worthy of you, flower of light, secrecy and silence, humility, reverence, innocence, heavenly, eternal love
Rose, white-color (American tradition)	happiness, security, traditional wedding flower
Rose, white-color (Asian tradition)	ultimate absence, death, death of the mother, ghosts
Rose, white-color, dried	death is preferable to loss of virtue
Rose, white-color, full-blown	I am worthy of you
Rose, white-color, withered	transient impressions, fleeting beauty, I am in despair
Roses, white- and coral-colors together	I desire you, you are heavenly
Roses, white- and red-colors together	unity, flower emblem of England, truth and love, bonding, harmony
Roses, white- and yellow-colors together	harmony
Rose, wild single	charming simplicity, poetry
Rose, withered	I would rather die
Rose, yellow-color	friendship, highest mark of distinction, congratulations, jealousy, joy, gladness, caring, platonic love, freedom, infidelity, the decrease of love
Roses, yellow- and red-colors together	happiness, celebration, joy, excitement, gaiety, congratulations
Roses, one yellow-color and eleven red-color	love and passion
Roses, yellow- and orange-colors together	passionate thoughts, enthusiasm, desire
Rose, York and Lancaster	conflict, war
Roses, a dozen	ultimate symbol of love, declaration of love
Roses, twenty-five	congratulations
Roses, fifty	unconditional love, pledge of eternal love
Roses, Crown of	reward of virtue
Rosebay, *Nerium*, *Oleander*	caution, beware, distrust

Rosebay Willow Herb, *Epilobium*	production, celibacy
Rosebud	beauty and youth, a heart innocent of love, you are young and beautiful, confession of love
Rosebud, unopened	unawakened love
Rosebud, pink-color	a young girl, beauty, gentleness, grace
Rosebud, Moss	confession of love
Rosebud, red-color	innocent hope, young and beautiful, pure and lovely
Rosebud, white-color	a heart untouched by love, purity, girlhood
Rosemary	devotion, fidelity, remembrance, wisdom, commitment, intellect, healing balm, constancy, stimulates healthy thinking and promotes well-being, your presence refreshes, good faith, fidelity
Rose of Sharon, *Alethea frutex*, *Syrian Mallow*	consumed by love, delicate beauty, beautiful, persuasion
Rowan, *Mountain Ash*, Mountainash Tree, Witchwood Tree	ambition, healing, empowerment, divination, tree of life, treachery, prudence, protection, with me you are safe, purification
Rudbeckia	justice, impartiality, love conquers all
Rue	clear vision, grace, repentance, can also mean disdain, fertility, manners, purification
Rush, *Juncus*	docility, navigation
Ryegrass	vice, changeable disposition

S

Safflower	marriage, welcome
Saffron	beware of excess, voluptuousness, you are perfectly lovely, do not abuse, mirth, laughter
Saffron Crocus	mirth
Saffron, Meadow, *Colchicum*	my happiest days are past
Sage	domestic virtue, skill, wisdom, greatest wisdom and respect, long life, gratitude, esteem, strength
Sage, Jerusalem, *Philomis*	earthly delights, pride of ownership
Sage, Mexican	eloquence, spectacular
Sage, Pineapple	esteem, hospitality, happy home

Sage, purple-leaf	gratitude
Sage, Russian, *Perovskia*	knowledge and wisdom
Sage, White*	protection, health, purification of space, eliminates negative energy
Sage, Wild, *Candy Kisses, Hemizygia**	cheerful, tenderness, sparkling personality, light-hearted, lively
Sainfoin, *Holy Clover*	you confuse me, agitation
Saintpaulia, *African Violet*	faithfulness
Salad Burnet	a merry heart, happy mood
Salal, *Gaultheria shallon*	zest, divine healing
Salvia	respect
Salvia, red-color	energy
Salvia, blue-color	wisdom, I think of you
Sambac, *Arabian Jasmine, Indian Jasmine*	attraction, I attach myself to you, attachment, love, fidelity, devotion, dedication
Sambucus, *Elderberry*	compassion, kindness
Sand Verbena, *Abronia*	delicacy, refinement
Sandalwood*	extravagantly suitable in an endeavor, highest mark of honor, spiritual empowerment, seductive, provocative, calmness in meditation
Sardony	irony
Satin Flower, *Godetia*	fascination, sincerity, love flower
Saxifraga, *London-Pride*	frivolity, fun, gaiety, lightheartedness
Scabiosa, *Pincushion*	admiration, widowhood, comfort in loss of someone
Scabiosa autopurpruea, *Black Mourning Bride, Mourning Bride Scabiosa*	I have lost all, unfortunate attachment
Scarlet Lobelia, *Cardinal Flower*	distinction
Schinus, *California Pepper Tree*	religious enthusiasm, sweetness, beauty, wit
Scilla, *Squill, Siberian Squill*	sympathy, patience, impressionable, lonely
Scotch Fir	elevation
Scotch Thistle	retaliation
Scrubbay, *Persea borbonia, Redbay, Swampby, Tisswood*	memory

Sea-Bindweed	uncertainty
Sea Holly, *Eryngium*	attraction
Sea Lavender, *Statice, Limonium*	never ceasing remembrance, sympathy, lasting beauty, dauntlessness
Sedum, *Stonecrop*	welcome, tranquility
Sempervivum, *Aeonium, Echevaria, Hens and Chicks, Houseleek, Succulents*	long life, vivacity, domestic economy, welcome home, resilience, robust
Senecio succulent species, *Blue Chalk Sticks, String of Bananas, String of Pearls**	companionship, harmony, understanding, engaging conversations, curiosity, occasionally spicy personality
Sensitive Plant, *Mimosa, includes Mimosa Tree, Persian Silk Tree*	sensibility, delicate feelings, prudery, secret, chastity, bashful modesty, secret love, fastidious, exquisite
Senvy, *Mustard Plant*	smart, indifference
Sequoia	long life, vast wisdom, perspective, health, protection, growth, durability, longevity, valor, enlightenment, eternity
Service Berry	harmony, agreement, prudence
Shamrock, *Oxalis, trifolium dubium*	Ireland, lightheartedness, luck, loyalty, wit
Shepherd's Purse	I offer you my all
Shrimp Plant, *Justicia brandegeana, Brazilian Plume*	perfection of female loveliness
Silene, *Red Catchfly*	youthful love, sun-beamed eyes
Silphium, *Compass Flower*	faith
Silverbell Tree, *Carolina Silverbell, Helesia Carolina**	surprise, epiphany, contentment, good fortune, prosperity, wonderment
Silver Fir	what you seek shall be found
Silver King, *Artemisia*	dignity, power, silver moonlight, sentimental recollections, unceasing remembrance, happiness
Silver Kochia, *Bassia**	adaptable, rugged for survival, resilient, orderly
Silverweed, *Argentina* or *Argentine, Silverleaf*	naiveté, timidity, simplicity
Siskiyou Pink, *Bee Blossom, Gaura, Wand Flower**	refreshing personality, exhilarating, lively, ability, intellect
Slipper Flower, *Calceolaria, Lady's Purse, Pocketbook Flower*	keep this for my sake

Sloe, *Blackthorn*	difficulty, death, unexpected or sudden change, I have changed radically, insouciance, transition
Smilax	loveliness and constancy
Smoke Bush, *Smoke Tree, Venetian Sumac*	generous, plentiful, opulent, generous in spirit, radiant and dreamy, splendor, intellectual excellence, adoration
Snapdragon	strength, gracious lady, power of will, presumption, coarseness, incivility, freedom
Sneezeweed, *Helenium*	tears
Sneezewort	freedom
Snowball Viburnum, *Guelder Rose*	good news, winter, age
Snowbell, Japanese, *Styrax japonicum**	good fortune, health, encouragement, blessing
Snowberry	heavenly thoughts
Snowdrop, *Galanthus*	hope, friendship, support, consolation, refinement, a friend in adversity
Snowflake, *Leucojum, Summer Snowflake*	herald of spring, purity, hope
Solidago, *Solidaster, Goldenrod*	encouragement, precaution, good fortune, protection
Solanum, *Potato Vine, Purple Robe Bush*	loneliness, smile, true
Solomon's Seal, *Polygonatum*	secret
Sorrel, wood	maternal love, secret sweetness, parental affection, joy
Southernwood	bantering, jest, pain
Spanish Jasmine, *Jasminum grandiflorum*	sensuality, separation, I think you're sexy
Sparaxis, *Harlequin Flower*	one tear, the harlequin, tears of a clown
Spearmint	warm sentiment, virtue, protection
Speedwell, *Veronica*	female fidelity, fidelity, I remain faithful
Speedwell, Germander, *Bird's-eye Speedwell*	facility, the more I see you, the more I love you
Spider Flower, *Cleome*	elope with me, not so bad as I seem
Spider Plant, *Anthericum*	antidote

Spiderwort, *Wandering Jew, Tradescantia, Virginia Spiderwort*	felicity, happiness, transient friendships
Spiked Willow Herb	pretension
Spindle Tree, *Euonymus*	long life, your image is engraved on my heart
Spiranthes, *Lady's-Tresses*	bewitching grace
Spirea	conceit, victory
Spruce	farewell, eternal hardiness, endurance, symbol of north and cold
Spurge, *Euphorbia*	purification, protection, persistence, welcome
Squill, *Scilla, Siberian Squill*	sympathy, patience, impressionable, lonely
St. John's Wort, *Hypericum*	protection, animosity, you are a prophet, superstition, originality
Stachys byzantina, *Lamb's Ears*	softness, support, surprise
Star of Bethlehem	hope, atonement, reconciliation, purity, idleness, harvest
Starwort, *Aster*	healthy emotions, love and contentment
Starwort, White Star and Late varieties	welcome to a stranger, afterthoughts, healthy emotions
Statice, *Sea Lavender, Limonioum*	never ceasing remembrance, sympathy, lasting beauty, dauntlessness
Stephanotis, *Floradora*	wedding, marital happiness, desire to travel
Sticky Monkey Flower, *Diplacus, Bush Monkey Flower**	I'm stuck on you, tenacious affection, let's stick together, prevalent fondness, universal love
Stirling Range Wax Flower, *Chamelaucium, Wax Flower, Geraldton Wax Flower*	riches, wealth, lasting love, patience, happy marriage
Sticklewort, *Agrimony, Church Steeples*	gratitude, thankfulness, recognition
Stock, *Gillyflower*	lasting beauty, promptness, bonds of affection, happy life, you'll always be beautiful to me
Stock, red-color	boredom
Stock, ten-week	promptness, promptitude
Stokes Aster, *Stokesia laevis**	refreshing friendships, extraordinary character, unique and distinquished personality
Stonecrop, *Sedum*	tranquility, welcome
Straw	agreement, united

Straw, Broken	rupture of a contract, quarrel, contention
Straw Flower	agreement
Strawberry	goodness, perfect goodness, esteem, love, perfume
Strawberry Begonia	cleverness
Strawberry Tree, *Arbutus, Madrone, Madrona*	esteem and love, thee only do I love, you are my only love
String of Bananas, *Blue Chalk Sticks, Senecio succulent species, String of Pearls**	companionship, harmony, understanding, engaging conversations, curiosity, occasionally spicy personality
String of Pearls, *Blue Chalk Sticks, Senecio succulent species, String of Bananas*	companionship, harmony, understanding, engaging conversations, curiosity, occasionally spicy personality
Styrax japonicus, *Japanese Snowbell**	good fortune, health, encouragement, blessing
Succory, *Chichorium, Chicory*	frugality, economy
Succulents, *Aeonium, Echeverias, Hens and Chicks, Houseleek, Sempervivum*	long life, vivacity, domestic economy, welcome home, resilience, robust
Sumac, Venetian, *Smoke Bush, Smoke Tree*	generous, plentiful, opulent, generous in spirit, radiant and dreamy, splendor, intellectual excellence, adoration
Sumac, Wild	I shall survive the change, splendid misery
Summer Snowflake, *Leucojum, Snowflake*	herald of spring, purity, hope
Summer Sweet, *Clethra, Sweet Pepperbush**	generous, favorable, brave, talented
Sun Cups, *Sun Drops, Evening Primrose, Oenothera*	happiness, happy love, sometimes inconstancy, mildness
Sundew, Round-leafed, *Drosera*	surprise
Sunflower, *Helianthus*	adoration, loyalty, you are splendid, best wishes, false riches, pride, my eyes only see you, haughtiness

The sunflower can represent false riches because however abundant one's material life is, you cannot render them truly rich if they are poor in spirit.

There are over a hundred types of oregano (Origanthum majorana).
Sweet marjoram is just one variety.

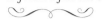

Sunflower, Dwarf	your devout adorer
Sunflower, Oxeye, *False Sunflower, Heliopsis* *	easygoing, subtleness, quiet, solitude, restful
Swainsona, *Darling Pea* *	bold yet graceful, a lady in every way, resilient, graceful beauty, consistently beautiful
Swallow-wort, *Asclepias, Butterfly Weed, Milkweed*	hope in misery, medicine, cure for heartache, let me go
Swampby, *Persea borbonia, Scrubbay, Redbay, Tisswood*	memory
Sweet Alyssum	worth beyond beauty, excellence beyond beauty, exemplary modesty, tranquility
Sweet Basil	good luck, best wishes, I send sweet wishes
Sweet Briar Rose, *American*	simplicity
Sweet Briar Rose, *European Eglantine, Rosa rubiginosa*	I wound to heal, poetry, a poetic person
Sweet Flag, *Wild Iris*	fitness and strength
Sweet Marjoram, *Oregano*	blushes, happiness, mirth, consolation, joy, kindness, courtesy, distrust
Sweet Pea	delicate pleasures, departure, tender memory, good-bye, blissful pleasure, thank you for a lovely time, a meeting, weakness
Sweet Pea, everlasting	lasting pleasure, an appointed meeting
Sweet Pea Shrub, *Polygala*	hermitage
Sweet Pepperbush, *Clethra, Summer Sweet* *	generous, favorable, brave, talented
Sweet Rocket, *Queen's Rocket, Dame's Rocket, Hesperis matronalis*	fashionable, you are the queen of coquettes!, evening, evening star, danger, rivalry
Sweet Sultan	felicity, happiness
Sweet William, *Dianthus barbatus, Pink*	love, affection, boldness, pure affection, classic love flower, childhood, memory, grant me one smile, perfection, finesse

Sweet Woodruff, *Galium*	humility, patience
Sweetspire, *Itea virginica, Virginia Sweetspire**	you radiate kindness, dazzling personality
Sweetshrub, *Calycanthus, Carolina Allspice*	benevolence
Sweetvetch, *Hedysarum*	agitation
Sycamore	growth and persistence, curiosity, hopes and cares
Syriacus, common garden Hibiscus	gentle (Japanese tradition, Hanakotoba), delicate beauty, old royalty (Pacific Island tradition), immortality (Korean tradition) tropical love flower, consumed by love, celebration flower (Malaysian tradition)
Syrian Mallow, *Alethea frutex, Rose of Sharon*	consumed by love, delicate beauty, beautiful, persuasion
Syringa, *Lilac*	beauty, love, youth, earliest first love, fraternal love, memory, humility, pride, confidence, you shall be happy yet, do you still love me?

T

Tamarix, *Tamarisk Tree*	crime, don't do me wrong
Tanacitum, *Feverfew (and hybrids)*	good health, warmth, you light up my life, protection
Tansy	resistance, I declare war against you, I resist you, stays miscarriages
Tare, *Vetch*	vice
Tea Tree, *Leptospermum, Manuka*	healing, strong health
Teasel, *Dipscaus*	misanthropy
Tendrils (any plant with tendrils)	ties that bind
Thalictrum, *Meadow Rue*	divination
Thistle	austerity, independence, nobility, harshness
Thornapple, general	I dreamed of thee
Thornapple, *Datura, Moon Flower, Jimsonweed*	delusive beauty, disguise, deceitful charms
Thorns on a branch	severity, rigor

Thrift, *Armeria*	sympathy
Throatwort, *Trachelium*	neglected beauty
Thryptomene, *Calcynia, Baeckea imbricata and grandiflora, Grampiens Heath Myrtle, Calynia, Heath Myrtle**	sustenance, adversity, opulence, abundance
Thyme	activity, bravery, courage, ensures good sleep, cuisine
Thyme, wild	thoughtlessness
Tibouchina urvilleana, *Glory Flower, Princess Flower*	glorious beauty, glory
Tigridia, *Tiger Flower, Jockey's Cap*	protection against cruelty, occasionally cruelty, for once may pride befriend me!
Tisswood, *Persea borbonia, Redbay, Scrubbay, Swampbay*	memory
Toad Flax, *Wild Antirrhinum*	presumption
Trachelium, *Throatwort*	neglected beauty
Tradescantia, *Spiderwort, Virginia Spiderwort, Wandering Jew*	felicity, happiness, transient friendships
Touch-me-not	impatience, impatience for love
Traveler's Joy, *Clematis vitalba*	rest, safety
Tree Mallow, *Lavatera*	sweet disposition
Trefoil, *Bird's Foot Trefoil*	revenge
Tremella, *Fungi*	resistance
Trifolium dubium, *Shamrock, Oxalis*	Ireland, lightheartedness, luck, loyalty, wit
Trifolium repens, *Four-Leaf Clover, Oxalis acetosella*	faith, hope, luck, love; when given to another: luck be with you, be mine; when given to a lover: you belong to each other
Trillium, *Wake Robin, Birthroot*	modest ambition, modest beauty
Triodanis perfoliata, *Venus' Looking-Glass*	flattery, ornament
Trollius, *Globe Flower*	solitude, generosity, gratitude
Trollius, *King-cups*	desire for riches
Triptilion spinosum	be prudent
Truffle, *Fungi (ground)*	surprise

Trumpet Flower, Ash-leafed, *Bigonia radicans*	separation
Trumpet Flower, *Trumpet Vine*, *Campsis radicans*	fame
Tritonia, *Flame Freesia, Blazing Star*	the weather vane, I am yours in all seasons
Tuberose	dangerous love, voluptuousness, risky pleasures, sweet voice, *le plus loin, le plus cher* (the farther away, the dearer)
Tulip	charity, fame, happy years, memory, declaration of love, famous, perfect lover, flower emblem of Holland, honesty
Tulip, budding	literary debut, best wishes for your new venture
Tulip, pink-color	dreaminess, imagination, love
Tulip, pink and purple shades	rural happiness, country charms
Tulip, Poplar Tree	fame, retirement, rural happiness, among the noblest
Tulip, red-color	declaration of ardent love, fame, believe me, my perfect love, reclamation of love
Tulip, variegated	beautiful eyes, your eyes are beautiful, enchantment, there is sunshine in your smile
Tulip, white-color	lost love
Tulip, yellow-color	sunshine in your smile, perfect love, lovely and majestic charms, hopeless love
Tulip Tree, *Saucer Magnolia*	bonds of love, fame
Turk's Cap Mallow, *Achania malvaviscus*, *Wax Mallow*	reserve
Turnip Blossom	help will come for you
Turnsole, *Indian Heliotrope*	intoxicated with joy, intoxication of love
Turtlehead, *Chelone*	pleasure without alloy
Tussilago, *Coltsfoot*	justice
Tweedia	hearts that believe in each other, blissful love

Tweedia

U

Ulmus, *American Elm*	dignity, grace, protection, patriotism, vigor
Urtica dioica, *Nettles*	slander, you are spiteful, you are cruel, don't sting me

V

Vaccinium, *Whortleberry*	treachery, treason
Valerian, Red	accommodating disposition, drunk and blowsy, readiness, facility
Valerian, Greek	rupture
Venus Fly Trap	caught at last, duplicity, deception
Venus' Looking-Glass, *Triodanis perfoliata*	flattery, ornament
Verbascum, *Common Mullein*	good nature, take courage, health
Verbena, *Vervain*	faithfulness, sensibility, sensitivity, fertility, marriage, pray for me, enchantment
Verbena, Lemon	responsibility
Verbena, pink-color	family union
Verbena, purple-color	I pray (weep) for you, regret
Verbena, Sand, *Abronia*	delicacy, refinement
Verbena, scarlet-color	sensibility, unite against evil, tender and quick emotion
Verbena, white-color	guileless, pray for me, pure, honesty
Verbena, Wild	good fortune, enchantment, superstition
Vernal Grass	poor but happy
Veronica, *Speedwell*	female fidelity, fidelity, I remain faithful
Vervain, *Verbena*	faithfulness, sensibility, sensitivity, fertility, marriage, pray for me, enchantment
Vervain, Blue, *Volkamenia*	may you be happy
Vetiver	tranquility, grounding
Vetch, *Tare*	I cling to thee, shyness
Viburnum, Snowball, *Guelder Rose*	winter, age, good news

Viburnum tinus, *Laurustinus*	I die if I am neglected
Vines, all sorts	intoxication, drunkenness, charity
Vine Lilac, *Coral Pea, Happy Wanderer, Hardenbergia**	spirited, happiness, capability, ingenuity
Violet, general, *Sweet Violet*	faithfulness, sweet beauty, I return your love, modesty, simplicity, love, prudery
Violet, blue-color	youthful innocence, watchfulness, hope, calming, love, I'll always be true
Violet, double	reciprocal friendship
Violet, Ivy, *Ivy-leafed Violet, Trailing Violet*	knots, knots of love
Violet, Parma	let me love you!
Violet, purple-color	thoughts of you, faithfulness, love, loyalty
Violet, vines or runner trails	bonds, knots of love
Violet, white-color	let's take a chance on happiness, I'll always be true, purity, candor, modesty, innocence, purity of sentiment
Violet, yellow-color	love of country, modesty, faithfulness, induces sleep, rural happiness, country charms, modest worth, perfect beauty
Violet, African, *Saintpaulia*	faithfulness
Virginia Cowslip	divinity
Virginia Creeper, *Ampelopsis quinquefolia, also includes Porcelain Vine, Woodbine*	I cling to you both in sunshine and shade, fraternal love, shyness
Virginia Spiderwort, *Spiderwort, Tradescantia, Wandering Jew*	felicity, happiness, transient friendships
Virginia Sweetspire, *Sweetspire, Itea virginica**	you radiate kindness, dazzling personality
Virgin's Bower, *Clematis*	love of brother, sister, sons, or daughters
Viscaria	will you dance with me?
Vitex, *Agnus castus, Chaste Tree*	coldness, living without love
Volkamenia, *Blue Vervain*	may you be happy

Violet

W

Wake Robin, *Trillium, Birthroot*	modest ambition, modest beauty
Wallflower, *Gillyflower*	lasting beauty, fidelity in aversity, promptness, luxury
Walnut	intellect, strength of mind, healing and protection, stratagem
Walnut Tree, *Watcher by the Wayside*	never despair
Wand Flower, *Bee Blossom, Gaura, Siskiyou Pink**	refreshing personality, exhilarating, lively, ability, intellect
Wandering Jew, *Spiderwort, Tradescantia, Virginia Spiderwort*	felicity, happiness, transient friendships
Watcher by the Wayside, *Walnut Tree*	never despair
Water Lily	purity of the heart, beauty, wisdom
Water Lily, white-color	eloquence and elegance
Water Lily, yellow-color	growing indifference
Watermelon	bulkiness
Wax Flower, *Chamelaucium, Stirling Range Wax Flower, Geraldton Wax Flower*	riches, wealth, lasting love, patience, happy marriage
Wax Plant, *Hoya*	susceptibility, sculptured loveliness, constancy, pure loveliness
Wax Mallow, *Achania malvaviscus, Turk's Cap*	reserve
Wax Myrtle, *Bayberry*	good luck, instruction, discipline, duty
Wheat Stalk	riches
Whin, *Gorse, Furze*	enduring affection, love for all occasions, can also mean anger
White Mullein	good nature
White Oak	independence
White Poplar, *Abele*	time
Whortleberry, *Vaccinium*	treachery, treason
Willow	freedom, friendship, serenity, strongly healing feminine aspects, forsaken

Willow, French	bravery and humanity
Willow, Peppermint, *Agonis, Burgundy Willow, Willow Myrtle**	grace, poise, versatility, attraction, balance
Willow, Pussy	friendship, recovery from illness
Willow, Water	freedom
Willow, Weeping	mourning, sadness, bravery, forsaken love, melancholy, bitter sorrow, forsaken
Willow Myrtle, *Peppermint Willow, Agonis, Burgundy Willow**	grace, poise, versatility, attraction, balance
Windflower, *Anemone*	sincerity, truth, abandonment, forsaken, expectation, anticipation, symbol of love
Winged Seeds, all sorts	messengers, spirit message from nature
Winter Cherry, *Chinese Lanterns, Withania somnifera*	deception
Wintergreen	harmony
Winter Greenery	immortality, renewal, survival and prosperity through adversity
Wisteria	daughter's sweetness, welcome stranger, cordial welcome, I cling to thee, your friendship is agreeable to me
Witch Hazel	a spell, inspiration, mysticism, a spell is upon me
Withania somnifera, *Winter Cherry, Chinese Lanterns*	deception
Woad, *Asp of Jerusalem, Dyer's Woad, Isatis tinctoria*	modest merit
Wolfsbane, *Aconite, Monkshood, Aconitum napellis, Helmet Flower, Turk's Cap, Friar's Cap*	misanthropy, treachery, poisonous words, symbol of crime, an enemy in disguise, chivalry, knight-errantry
Woodbine, *Ampelopsis quinquefolia, also includes Porcelain Vine, Virginia Creeper*	I cling to you both in sunshine and shade, fraternal love, shyness
Woodruff	sweet humility
Wood Sorrel	joy, maternal tenderness
Wooly Bush*	tenacious but subdued, gentleness, tolerant, forgiving
Wormwood, *Absinthe, Artemisia absinthium*	absence, not to be discouraged, affection, bitterness, comfort, protection for travelers

X

| Xanthium, *Cocklebur* | pertinacity, rudeness |
| Xeranthemum, *Eternal Flower, Everlasting Daisy* | unfading remembrance, cheerful in adversity, eternity, immortality |

Y

Yarrow, *Achillea*	cure for heartache, heals wounds, health, sorrow, war, to dispel melancholy and heartache
Yellow rose of Texas, *Kerria japonica, Easter Rose, Japanese Kerria, Pleniflora***	pleasant through the years, mature grace, perpetual beauty, be tough but stay beautiful, long beautiful
Yerba Mate, *Ilex paraguariensis***	friendship, encouragement, cordiality, energy, mental clarity, upbeat happiness, communal happiness
Yew	penitence, sorrow, transformation, reincarnation, death and rebirth, great age, good shield, protection
Yucca, *Adam's Needle*	natural charms, abundant and hardy life

Yarrow

Z

Zantadeschia, *Calla Lily, Arum Lily*	feminine modesty, loveiness, pure elegance, magnificent beauty, with me you are safe
Zephyr Flower	sincerity, symbol of love, expectation
Zephyranthes, *Rain Lily*	expectation, fond caresses
Zinnia	kind thoughts of absent friends, I miss you, absence
Zinnia, magenta-color	lasting affection
Zinnia, mixed colors	thinking of an absent friend
Zinnia, scarlet-color	constancy
Zinnia, white-color	goodness
Zinnia, yellow-color	daily remembrance

QUICK-START OCCASIONS DIRECTORY

Use this chart to see some of the flowers that are most representative of a particular occasion. Note that this list is designed to help you select flowers for specific occasions, but not to provide a recipe. For full recipes, see the completed posies on pages 38–121.

ANNIVERSARY

Honeysuckle: *generous and devoted affection, chains of love*	Bergamot: *your wiles are irresistible!*	Calla Lily: *magnificent beauty*
Baby's Breath: *everlasting love*	Magenta-color Zinnia: *lasting affection*	Quince Flower: *symbol of love*

BIRTHDAY

Coral Rose: *longevity*	Red Geranium: *comfort, health, protection*	Bells of Ireland: *whimsy, good luck, gratitude*
Lemon Balm: *fun*	Euonymus: *long-life*	Calendula: *health, joy, affection*

GET WELL

Chamomile: *health*	Ginger: *pleasant, warming*	Green Rose: *freshness, health*
Cedar: *strength*	Lemon Balm: *healing, relief*	Buttercup: *cheerfulness*

I MISS YOU

Cranberry: *cure for heartache*	Striped Rose: *warmth of heart*	Wormwood: *absence, protection for travelers*
White Poplar: *time*	Fern: *sincerity, shelter*	Gooseberry: *anticipation*

I'M SORRY

Purple Hyacinth: *I'm sorry, please forgive me*	Allspice: *compassion*	Peppermint: *warmth of feeling*
Rose of Sharon: *persuasion*	Weeping Willow: *sadness*	Flowering Almond: *hope, promise, thoughtfulness*

JUST BECAUSE

Lemon Mint: *cheerfulness, virtue*	Dogwood: *I admire your personality and social abilities*	Iris: *valued friendship*
Chocolate Cosmos: *simple pleasures*	Yellow Lily: *gaiety, happiness, purity of spirit*	Mugwort: *tranquility, happiness, peace*

MOTHER-TO-BE

Moss: *maternal love*	Freesia: *innocence, trust, thoughtfulness*	Elderberry: *compassion, kindness*
Goldenrod: *encouragement*	Dock: *patience*	Mountain Ash: *ambition*

FOR SISTERS

Virgin's Bower Clematis: *love of sister*	Grevillea: *steadfastness, loyalty*	Birch: *graciousness*
Cherry Blossom: *feminine beauty*	Delphinium: *sweetness, well-being*	Begonia: *highly popular*

SYMPATHY

Lamb's Ears: *support, comfort*	Oak: *strength, healing*	White Rose: *eternal love, heavenly, peace*
Peppermint: *warmth of feeling*	Balm: *sympathy, relief from sadness*	Pieris: *happy thoughts*

THANK YOU

Dahlia: *gratitude*	Clethra: *generous*	Campanula: *aspiring*
Azalea: *gratitude*	Chervil: *sincerity*	White Zinnia: *goodness*

⇒ QUICK-START SENTIMENTS DIRECTORY ⇐

Use the sentiments directory to quickly find flowers that are representative of a certain feeling, sentiment, or emotion.

HAPPINESS Oregano, Lavender, Chamomile, Jack-in-the-Pulpit, Baby's Breath, Bottle Brush

SORROW White Rose, Adonis (Crowfoot), Aloe, Balm, Scabiosa, Weeping Willow

LOVE Red Rose, Orchid, Myrtle, Rose Acacia, Sweet William, Carnation

FRIENDSHIP Alstromeria, Pine Boughs, Yellow Rose, Snowdrop, Willow, Acacia

BEAUTY Stock, Wallflower, Calla Lily, Bougainvillea, Camellia, Pink Carnation

GRATITUDE Campanula, Cotton, Abelia, Dahlia, Azalea, Peach Rose, Purple-leaf Sage

HOPE Hawthorne, Snowdrop, White Chrysanthemum, Four-leafed Clover, Crocus, Iris

LUCK Lavender, Forsythia, Heath, White Heather, Hydrangea, Shamrock

WELCOME Euphorbia, Juniper, Safflower, Stonecrop Sedum, Peony

HEALTH Feverfew, Bachelor Buttons, Green Rose, White Sage, Chamomile, Purple Coneflower

FESTIVITY & GOOD CHEER Baby's Breath, Bunch of Daffodils, Delphinium, White Cosmos, Geum, Yellow Rose

SYMPATHY Balm, Thrift, Harebell, Snowdrop, Statice, Flowering Reed, Yarrow

GRACE Rue, Jasmine, Abutilon, Elm, White Geranium, Pink Rose

RESOURCE DIRECTORY

SUPPLIES AND EQUIPMENT

www.durokon.com: For high quality (Zenport) clippers and trimming shears. These are wonderful for working with tiny blooms on posies.

www.jamaligarden.com: For clippers, ribbons, and posy vases.

www.gardeners.com: For clippers, watering cans, and other garden supplies.

www.save-on-crafts.com: For cloth covered floral stem wire (for making bows), flower food, binding tape, and twine.

www.fiftyflowers.com: For various floristry supplies

PACKAGING

Containers

It doesn't take very long to accumulate a good amount and variety of posy containers. Once you learn what size works best (see page 138), you'll begin to keep a watchful eye when you're out and about and before you know it you'll have some on hand always.

Discount stores such as Ross and Marshalls are great resources for containers. Sometimes you can find boxes of dessert dishes, or ice cream cups, which can be ceramic or glass, or crystal. These make wonderful posy containers because they are usually footed with the desired diameter of 2 to 3 inches.

Antique shops may have a good choice of mugs and teacups. A warning about teacups though: for several years I collected the most exquisite vintage teacups for my posies. However, they are very difficult to use for posies, as they are so shallow. If you want to use teacups, you'll need to cut your stems very short, and then really fan out your posy on the edges so that there is coverage along the lip, or top line, of the cup. The sentiment tag looks fantastic tied to the handle of the teacup with a ribbon.

Good Will and other recycle and thrift stores will usually provide a good selection of containers.

You can also purchase containers online from these websites:

www.jamaligarden.com: This site has some beautiful options, including goblets!

www.wholesaleflowersandsupplies.com: Their mini milk glass vase is perfect for smaller posies

www.shopmadonnainn.com: These are the famed Madonna Inn goblets I used for the posies on pages 2, 8, 40, 53, 64, and 104. These are my all-time favorite containers to use!

www.save-on-crafts.com

www.wayfair.com: A nice selection of goblets

Sentiment Tags

As mentioned earlier, without at least a note, but preferably a sentiment tag, your posy is a flower arrangement, a beautiful and thoughtful flower arrangement yes, but a posy is not a posy without a card of some sort with a description of the flowers and their meanings. I have listed some sources for creating sentiment tags here for you, but please, use what you feel would make a good sentiment tag or note card to attach to your posy. It doesn't have to be elaborate and can even be the cutout front of an old Hallmark card. The idea is that sentiment tags are the most important aspect of a posy, and I would like you to get as creative as you feel you want to, or as simple as you need.

My website (teresasabankaya.com) is a fabulous source for your sentiment tags. There are several options for downloadable pre-designed tags where all you have to do is insert your text, print on card stock, and cut it out. There are also added resources and inspirational ideas for your sentiment tag designs.

Besides card stock papers that you can use in your printer, there are many paper sources to create the sentiment tag. Any craft store will have a good choice of papers for scrapbooking, and usually will have some shipping tags too. Shipping tags work wonderfully for sentiment tags and they're already shaped nicely, and they will have a hole punched already for your ribbon.

It's fun to get a paper pack from Emma's Paperie (www.emmaspaperie.com) with beautiful illustrations and drawings. You would write your sentiments on the blank side and embellish to coordinate with the paper design on the back. These are usually a card stock weight and work nicely for a nicely decorated sentiment tag.

If you own a die cutter, this site offers a wide array of die cuts that are perfect for sentiment tags. You can also use stencils to create borders and embellishments. It is incredible the things you can do with your sentiment tags. They can lend a very beautiful and artistic touch to your posies if you want, or they can be simple and elegant too.

If you're into scrapbooking (www.scrapbook.com), and have a die cutter, you can make some incredibly beautiful sentiment tags! You can find all sorts of tag materials on this site, including various die cut shapes and a large selection of paper and card stock. The galleries can provide great inspiration and ideas to embellish your tags with all sorts of fun stuff, from ribbons and rosettes to tin hearts.

Shipping tags, gift tags, stamping supplies at www.michaels.com.

In the craft supplies and tools section of Etsy (www.etsy.com), there are numerous shops that stock items that would be good to embellish tags such as stamps, cutouts, and stickers.

Ribbons

I am a ribbon fanatic! Ribbons make a posy a pretty package. Unless you've heavily embellished your sentiment tag, in which case you can use a simple decorative twine, you will need beautiful ribbon to present your posy. The best width to use to make and pretty bow and to hang your tag from is ⅜ inch. If the ribbon is shear you can use a wider width due to its flexibility. Too wide of a ribbon that is not flexible and giving will rip the hanging hole punch.

> **Tinsel Trading (www.tinseltrading.com):** Originally located in Manhattan, this adorable shop is now located in Berkeley, California, and is my favorite place to go and browse some unique vintage ribbon and embellishments. The online store is well organized and stocked with ribbons (vintage and new), trims, embellishments, appliques, sequins, buttons, and more.

> **Save On Crafts (www.save-on-crafts.com):** Just ribbon, although sometimes they do have some items that would be pretty for embellishments.

> **Ribbon Resource (www.ribbonresource.com):** This is the retail outlet for May Arts Ribbon, which supplies some of my favorite ribbons to use for posies. Grosgrain ribbon is my favorite, and this site has it available here in some very beautiful color selections, along with stripes and other patterns. This site also has adhesive ribbons, which are a simple and quick way to add some pizzazz to your sentiment tags!

PLANTS

Of course, I love to support the local garden centers and nurseries, but there are times when plant catalogs can provide some very inspirational and sometimes new hybrids of old favorites. When the winter is set in, and you're seeing nothing but gray and white, these catalogs are a sight to behold and trigger your desire to be out of doors and in the garden again.

Bluestone Perennials (www.bluestoneperennials.com): I love good cutting shrubs, such as Abelia, or Deutzia, to use in my posies and floral designs. Bluestone's catalog is packed with amazing shrubs that I don't think to look for while at a garden center. Their website has a very handy Plant Finder tool that allows you to search the perfect plant for the color desired and/or growing condition. They have a beautiful specimen of Cimicifuga *ramose*, Black Bugbane (Cohosh) that I love using in posies.

Annie's Annuals (www.anniesannuals.com): I can't say enough good things about Annie's Annuals. This is my go-to for 4-inch annuals in the garden. I live about 2 hours from where they're located, but it is always worth the time spent going there. Some plants I have bought from here have lasted for more than 10 years! That's the beauty of annuals, and when you need to get your garden planted with flowers that keep on giving, year after year, this is the place to go. This is a good source for Chervil, meaning *sincerity*, which is great go-to plant for posies. This site is a colorful delight, and you'll get excited looking at all the color and whimsy, as well as a little story about each item that is offered.

Longfield Gardens (www.longfieldgardens.com): There is a nice selection of Caladium (*Great joy, Delight*) bulbs here, and they usually have some sort of special offerings and sales going on too. Also, the articles and "how-to" pages are a great help and you can often find great resources and learning from this site.

Monrovia Plants (www.shop.monrovia.com): You can buy plants online and have them shipped to your local garden center free of charge. What a handy detail! Monrovia is the leader in new plant introductions and here is a good example of why the language of flowers will continue to grow. This site is chock-full of the tried and true favorites, as well as a wide array of new introductions. The plants grown by Monrovia are always high quality and very healthy, with over 3,000 varieties to choose from, and the handy selection tool lets you choose your plants based on growing conditions and landscape needs and uses.

CUT FLOWERS

If you can grow some flowers for cutting that is the best! The idea of this book is to inspire you to get out into your garden and learn to use what you have growing to create posies. However, there will be times when you'll need to supplement your blooms with store-bought flowers when making a posy. There have been times when I only have complementary flowers and some greens and herbs, with no focal to be found in my own garden. In this case it's good to have some reliable resources lined up to buy your cut flowers.

Slow Flowers™ (www.slowflowers.com): I strongly believe in the importance of the American cut flower industry, and I am a huge advocate of sourcing local flowers. I have been committed since the first day of my business to use only locally grown flowers (if I couldn't grow them myself!), so you could say that I'm a pioneer of the Slow Flowers™ movement! Slow Flowers™ means to make a conscious choice, and a commitment to buying locally grown flowers. Since 1992, we have lost over 80 percent of our American flower farmers due to increased imports of South American grown flowers. And these days, it's easy to find locally grown flowers, and the Slow Flowers™ website is a very thorough resource to find flowers listed by category: Retail Flower Shop, Floral Studio, Supermarket Floral Department, Weddings/Events, Flower CSAs, or Flower Growers. You can even find a workshop or event to attend in your area.

Why buy local flowers?

- Almost 80 percent of our flowers are purchased from South America, Mexico, and the Netherlands. This has put a toll on the American flower farmer, reducing the number of American flower farms down to less than 20 percent of what it was in the 1980s. Importing flowers from South America and elsewhere produces a massive carbon footprint and the flowers often are doused in harmful pesticides.

- They smell better, and they are fresher. Imported flowers are usually cut up to a week prior to when you'll have them in your hands.

- U.S. flowers are grown with stricter, environmentally responsible growing methods.

- You are supporting your local farms and local economy.

Certified American Grown Flowers (www.americangrownflowers .org): Look for the Certified American Grown label on all your flowers, whether from the grocery store or your local flower shop. The Certified American Grown Flowers coalition is comprised of flower farmers throughout the nation providing consumers' confidence in the source of their flowers. The certification guarantees the bunches that you purchase are grown and assembled here in the US. Check the website for the fabulous Field to Vase dinners and try to attend one. They are really a lot of fun and always held in a beautiful setting.

The California Cut Flower Commission, or CCFC (if you are in California, you can utilize this resource at www.ccfc.org.): A state agency responsible for representing cut flower and greens farmers in California.

The Association of Specialty Cut Flower Growers (www.ascfg .org): The ASCFG has an extensive state by state directory of flower growers. Some growers may not have a retail outlet and only sell direct to florists or grocery store chains, but you can find out by sending a quick contact email or phone call to them.

Floret Flowers (www.floretflowers.com): Floret Farm's Collective directory will give you access to flower shops and flower farms throughout the world. The website and blog are highly informative with loads of how-to information including how to grow beautiful cut flowers as well as designing with cut flowers.

The British Flower Collective (www.thebritishflowercollective.com): An online directory of flower growers and floral designers that believe 'British is Best' when it comes to flowers. They are in England primarily, but can ship throughout the UK.

Other sources:

- Farmer's market

- If you're lucky enough, a flower market in your town or city

- Grower's Market or Co-op

- Supermarket Floral Department—*just remember to buy flowers with the Certified American Grown label.* Not all supermarket flowers are local, and not only are they imported flowers from South America, they are usually dipped in harmful pesticides and fungicides.

SEEDS

If you're an adventurous gardener, and you also want to really expand the availability of some unique flowering plants, vines, and herbs, then seeds are the way to go. Below are sources for seeds to purchase from catalogs, or online as indicated:

J.L. Hudson, Seedsman (www.jlhudsonseeds.net): Since 1911, Hudson operates an extensive seed bank with an unbelievable selection of seeds. I have ordered several times from Hudson—they have a highly unusual choice of seeds you cannot find elsewhere, and often the seeds are very rare. Seeds are available to order online, although there is no shopping cart. You'll have to select your seeds, then email to order, and pay via Paypal. You can also mail an order form (printable from the website) and send a check for payment. I am happy to support this business, as it is conscious of the need for saving heirloom and precious seeds, and of course, as are all plantsmen, up against the USDA with regard to small agriculture and seed-saving.

Botanical Interests (www.botanicalinterests.com): The seed packets from Botanical Interests offer beautiful artwork and are like mini-encyclopedias, too. They are very informative about each seed and how to germinate it, and about the plant's growth habit, harvest tips, and even recipes. Best of all, the seeds are non-GMO, which means Botanical Interests is using true heirloom seeds that have not been genetically modified. Yes, this is important for cut flowers too, not just food. As we continue to develop more hybrid strains of beautiful flowers and plants that grow stronger, taller, more prolific, etcetera, it is imperative to conserve our pure heirloom seeds too.

Renee's Garden (www.reneesgarden.com): A local hero where I live, Renee's Garden is an incredible resource for cut flowers to use in posies and for a lot of unique kitchen garden and edibles. They are absolutely a provider for not only non-GMO seeds, and also for pollinator friendly options, too. The website is incredibly resourceful, with a Gardening Resource section that is extensive, with how-to videos, inspirational planting themes, and everything you need to know about starting your garden from seed to harvest, and then some!

Floret Flowers (www.floretflowers.com): The seed selection at Floret is geared for a beautiful collection of cut flowers and some herbs. Floret is a farmer-florist business, so the seeds available are incredibly useful for growing many flowers for posies.

Eden Brothers (www.edenbrothers.com): A very informative site where you can find some unique heirloom seeds for herbs and flowers. You can find seeds for Maltese Cross (*religious enthusiasm, sweetness, beauty, wit*), which can be a workhorse flower in posies because of its conventional and handy sentiments.

ROUTLEDGE
A VICTORIAN F
NARY
THE MEANING OF
Scoble & Field
TUSSIE-MUSSIES
ALDINE ADAMICH LAUFER

BIBLIOGRAPHY

BOOK SOURCES

Connolly, Shane. *The Secret Language of Flowers*. New York: Rizzoli (2004).

Greenaway, Kate. *Language of Flowers*. London: George Routledge and Sons (1884).

Heilmeyer, Marina. *The Language of Flowers: Symbols and Myths*. Munich, London, New York: Prestel Verlag (2001).

Laufer, Geraldine Adamich. *Tussie Mussies: The Victorian Art of Expressing Yourself in the Language of Flowers*. New York: Workman Publishing Company (1993).

Lehner, Earnst, and Johanna Lehner. *Folklore and Symbolism of Flowers, Plants and Trees*. New York: Tudor Publishing Company (1960).

Okies, Leigh, and Lisa McGuinness. *Meaningful Bouquets*. San Francisco: Chronicle Books (2016).

Phillips, Henry. *Floral Emblems*. London: Saunders and Otley (1825).

Pickston, Margaret. *The Language of Flowers*. London: Michael Joseph Ltd (1968).

Seaton, Beverly. *The Language of Flowers: A History*. Charlottesville and London: University of Virginia Press (1995).

Seelye, Charles W. *The Language of Flowers and Floral Conversation*. Rochester, NY: Union and Advertiser Co's Print (1878).

Shoberl, Frederick L., Louise Cortambert, and Louis-Aimé Martin. *Flora Symbolica, or The language of flowers: with illustrative poetry*. Philadelphia: Lea & Blanchard (1848).

Tyas, Robert. *The Language of Flowers or, Floral Emblems of Thoughts, Feelings, and Sentiments*. New York: George Routledge and Sons (1875).

Waterman, Catharine. *Flora's Lexicon, an interpretation of The Language and Sentiment of Flowers*. Boston. Phillips, Sampson, and Company (1857).

Zarincbaf, Fariba. University of California Press. Retrieved 2011 from Subjects> History>Middle East History: https://content.ucpress.edu/chapters/11549.ch01.pdf

DIGITAL SOURCES

aggie-horticulture.tamu.edu/archives/parsons/publications/flowers/flowers.html

almanac.com

angelfire.com

archive.org/stream/languageflowers00martgoog#page/n24/mode/2up

bbc.com/news/science-environment-36230858

berkleycenter.georgetown.edu/posts/mono-no-aware-the-transience-of-life

botanical.com

buildingbeautifulsouls.com/symbols-meanings/flower-meanings-symbolism/narcissus-meaning-symbolism/#Victorian

bulbapedia.bulbagarden.net/wiki/Tweedia

Conkling, V. (2010). Smithsonian Gardens. Retrieved from Smithsonian Gardens: http://www.gardens.si.edu/collections-research/poetker-collection.html

daleharvey.com/Directory/articles-of-interest/LANGUAGE+OF+FLOWERS/Meaning +of+Flowers.html#H

drifttherapy.wordpress.com/2012/07/31/the-language-of-wild-flowers-2/

dvineflowers.ca/5-popular-winter-flowers-meanings

emptyvase.com/blog/the-ancient-history-of-flowers/

floriography.bernardyu.com/

flowermeaning.com

gardens.si.edu/collections-research/poetker-collection.html

h2g2.com/edited_entry/A5268035

interflora.co.nz/flowers/flower-meanings/

joellessacredgrove.com/language.html

Lady Mary Wortley Montagu, from The Turkish Embassy Letters (1763). (n.d.). Retrieved from www.wwnorton.com/college/english/nael/18century/topic_4/montagu.htm

languageofflowers.com

meaningfulmarriages.com/flowers-and-their-meanings/

medium.com/@TiffanyR/hanakotoba-the-japanese-language-of-flowers-9410aa14d7b5

metafilter.com/158324/The-language-of-flowers-spoken-in-forms-around-the-world

missouribotanicalgarden.org/PlantFinder/PlantFinderDetails.aspx?kempercode=d108

motherearthliving.com

muslimheritage.com/article/lady-montagu-and-introduction-smallpox-inoculation-england

notablekinklings.wordpress.com

perennial-gardens.com/flower-meanings.php

pioneerthinking.com/the-language-of-flowers-what-they-mean-l-z

powerflowers.com

proflowers.com

rosydawngardens.com

slideplayer.com/slide/9355928/

thegardenpages.com

thelanguagejournal.com/2012/10/hanakotoba-japanese-secret-language_18.html

zyanya.wikidot.com/the-language-of-flowers

INDEX OF POSY INGREDIENTS

ABOUT THE AUTHOR

Teresa Hannegan Sabankaya is the founder and creative director of Bonny Doon Garden Company in Santa Cruz, California, a business she began in 1999 by growing her own assortment of boutique cut flowers. Teresa is one of the most innovative floral designers in the San Francisco and Monterey Bay Area and has exhibited her floral art at numerous museums and flower shows including the *Bouquets to Art* exhibition at the De Young Museum in Golden Gate Park, the Monterey Museum of Art, and Filoli Mansion and Gardens (a National Trust Historic Site).

Her love of, or rather *obsession* with, the language of flowers spawned her creation of the modern-day posy. The posy is her favorite design in florals; a modern spin on a historic nosegay, these "little garden bouquets that tell a story" have a permanent place in her heart. This book was inspired by her desire to share such a beautiful and simple way to tell *your* story with flowers.

Teresa is an instructor of floral design and can be frequently seen leading workshops and presentations about flowers in many levels. Her Posy in Your Pocket presentations have been highly attended at the San Francisco Flower and Garden Show, the Monterey Home and Garden Expo, Filoli Estate, and many garden clubs and nurseries. Teresa is a pioneer of the Slow Flowers™ movement by her longstanding commitment to using her own organically grown, and other locally sourced flowers in her floral designs at her retail store and her wedding and event floral work.

Teresa is an Advanced Certified Green Gardener and a member of Slow Flowers™, Great Garden Speakers, Slow Weddings Network, and the California State Floral Association. She and her work have been featured in *Flower Confidential* by Amy Stewart, the PBS documentary *Botany of Desire* (based on the book by Michael Pollan), *New York Times*, *Elle*, CBS *Sunday Morning*, *Romantic Homes Magazine*, *Country Gardens Magazine*, *San Francisco Chronicle*, and elsewhere.

To learn more about the world of flowers, visit teresasabankaya.com and newlanguageofflowers.com and follow Teresa on Instagram, Facebook, and Twitter @teresasabankaya.